Sietas and its Ships (Part 2)

Bernard McCall

Although the J J Sietas yard was arguably best known for building cargo ships, its huge output included many other types of vessels including barges, tankers and roll on / roll off vessels. The **Stena Seafarer** was a good example and was one of three sisterships built in 1974/75 as Type 87. All three had a complex history. They were originally built for Stena Line to the company's "Stena Seaporter" design but they did not initially operate for Stena. The first two were sold to Pandoro and the third, named **Stena Trader** when her keel was laid, was launched as **Union Melbourne** for charter to Union Steamship of New Zealand upon completion. All three had various modifications during their careers. This example was lengthened at the Nobiskrug shipyard in Rendsburg in 1975 and in 1980, having been briefly renamed **Union Trader**, was further modified at South Shields with passenger accommodation being added. She emerged as **Puma** in 1980. She and her two sisterships then operated on the Fleetwood to Larne service. In 1998 she was renamed **European Seafarer**. Ironically they all came into Stena operation in 2004 when the route was purchased by Stena and this example was renamed **Stena Seafarer**. The photograph was taken as she arrived at Fleetwood on 16 May 2010. After closure of the route later in 2010, all three were sold to Russian owners. Renamed **Ant 2**, she and her sisters were reported to have been used in connection with the winter Olympics at Sochi in 2014 prior to recycling at Aliaga.

(Bernard McCall)

Introduction

The shipyard of J J Sietas is arguably one of the best-known in northern Europe. It was founded in 1635 and from its inception, the company was continuously owned by the founding family. This was the ninth generation by 2009. The first vessels were made out of wood but this changed to steel from the early 20th century. By 2009 the shipyard was experiencing financial difficulties due to rising steel prices, the rapid fall in demand for container ships and miscalculation of costs. The global recession led to cancelled orders and the shipyard's largest creditor, HSH Nordbank, took over management in early March 2009, the first time the company had been managed by someone outside of the founding family since 1635. The yard continued to experience financial problems until April 2014 when it became part of the Pella group, a Russian company owned by the Tsaturof family. The yard is now known as Pella Sietas Werft. Some of the consequences of the bankruptcy can be seen in the later types listed in this book.

It was in the mid-1950s when production was starting to increase that a decision was made to classify the vessels according to types. At first letters were used, so in 1955 six examples of the Type HG were built, named after the **Hertha Gerdau**. Type A and Type F also appeared before it was decided to adopt a numerical scheme beginning with **Karin** in 1958. This scheme has continued to the present day. It should be understood that the yard was building several different types at the same time. Especially in the 1970s, it was unable to keep up with demand and several vessels were subcontracted to the Norderwerft shipyard in Hamburg which became part of the Sietas group in 1972. In this book we shall be concentrating on cargo ships but other types will also appear to illustrate the variety of ships that were built. Sietas also built fishing vessels and items of port infrastructure; these are not mentioned in this book.

Bernard McCall   Portishead   July 2021

Acknowledgements

This book could not have been written without the help of many individuals. A look at the photo credits proves how many people have been willing to provide assistance. I am grateful to all of them. I also extend my gratitude to the many people who have helped by answering specific questions. Two German books have been invaluable: *Die Typschiff der Sietas-Werft* by Gert Uwe Detlefsen and *Sietas Werft von 1635 - 2000* by Klaus Krummlinde.

Every effort has been made to minimise the number of errors in the book and in this context I want to express my appreciation to Gil Mayes and Richard Potter whose proof reading has been meticulous. I remain totally responsible for any mistakes and I apologise for these. Finally I must thank the staff of Gomer Press who have once again done a marvellous job in producing the book.

Front cover: In the late 1970s and 1980s, a small group of Sietas-built coasters were built for a very specific trade. This was the transport of china clay slurry from Fowey and Par in Cornwall to certain European destinations. Much more is written about these vessels on pages 40, 42 and 67. The vessels were operated by Rhein- Maas- und See- Schiffahrtskontor (RMS), a German company with its main office in Duisburg but with other offices and agencies serving the canal and river systems of Europe. RMS used vessels which they exclusively managed and which often were developed to meet the requirements of individual customers. This image, taken at Fowey on 29 August 1988, allows a comparison between **Pandor** (Type 104) and **Kirsten** (Type 128).

(Cedric Catt)

Back cover: Type 168 was the most successful type ever produced by Sietas and 52 ships were built to this design. The majority of the ships were built as basic Type 168 which were strengthened for winter navigation in the Baltic but were gearless. Like the earlier Type 160, they had a partial open hatch design and had capacity for 868TEU. As demand for container feeder services to the Baltic continued to grow, this type proved ideal and dominated the trade for several years. The **Anna Sophie Dede** was delivered as **Joanna Borchard** on 12 October 2001. Name changes saw her become **Holland Maas Antilles** (2004), **Anna Sophie Dede** (2006), **Judith Borchard** (2010), **Anna Sophie Dede** (2012) and **Moveon** (2016). She is seen approaching the Grünental bridge on the Kiel Canal on 12 August 2007.

(Dominic McCall)

The Type 83 represented a huge step forward in naval architecture and proved to be one of the most successful designs of the 1970s. Between 1973 and 1978, twenty examples were built with six different sub-classes being used. A new hull design was used featuring a flared bow section, a bulbous bow with bow thruster and a transom stern which replaced the cruiser stern of earlier designs. One of the six basic Type 83 ships was launched as *Francop* on 11 April 1974 and delivered on 17 May. In 1976 she was chartered by Manchester Liners and renamed *Manchester Faith*. Off charter in 1977 she became *Francop* but her charter was renewed so once again she was renamed *Manchester Faith* in 1977 and worked on the company's Mediterranean service linking Manchester to Valletta, Limassol, Ashdod and Haifa. Later changes of name saw her become *Casablanca* (1990), *OPDR Cartagena* (1997) and *Marianne* (1998). In mid-November 2003 she was sold, renamed *Ansai* and left Rotterdam on 22 December bound initially for Nouakchott in Mauritania before heading through the Mediterranean, Suez Canal and eventually Singapore. She returned to the eastern Mediterranean as *Tiger* in 2006 then *Arrow S* in 2007. She continues to trade in that area.

(Bernard McCall)

The Type 83a sub-group had a deeper draught and container capacity of 210 TEU compared to the 195 of the basic Type 83. They also had twin funnels. Only two examples were built, both for Peter Döhle. The first was launched on 14 June 1975 and delivered as *Diana* on 22 August. She was renamed *Diana II* in 1983. A sale to OPDR saw her renamed *Rabat* in 1988, this being changed to *OPDR Rabat* in 1997 when she was sold and chartered back to OPDR. Further sales saw her become *Koningshaven* in 1998 and *Hege* in 2001. On 14 June 2010, she was seen passing the Hook of Holland inbound to Rotterdam. By the end of that year she was working on the coast of North Africa and in the following year she was bought by owners in the Middle East and renamed *Altarek III*. There followed a series of sales and renamings that saw her become *Adnan H* (2013), *Chaar Sea* (2014), *Shnar K* and then *Haj Houryah* (2016) and *El Youssef* (2018). She was reported to be trading mainly between Tripoli (Lebanon) and Tartous (Syria) in autumn 2019 and was renamed *Manassa 2M* in December 2020.

(Darren Hillman)

Five examples of the Type 83 design were built in two batches for the Moroccan national shipping company. The first batch of three was designated Type 83b and the ships were equipped to carry more refrigerated containers than the basic Type 83 as they were intended to work in the fruit export trade from Morocco to northern Europe. The last of the three was **Ouirgane** which was launched on 28 October 1975 and delivered on 12 December. Sold in 2002 she was renamed **Abnett Snow** and became **Snow White** in 2007. We see her in the Bosphorus on 5 July 2016. Carrying a bagged cargo, there would have been no requirement for her reefer capacity on this voyage. This sub-group reverted to a single funnel. She was delivered for recycling at Aliaga in late May 2019.

(Simon Smith)

The five vessels in the Type 83c sub-group have identical dimensions to those in 83a but they are multipurpose unlike the dedicated container carriers in 83a. They are also ice-classed. Ordered by Gerd Ritscher, this vessel was launched on 26 April 1976 as *Jan* and delivered on 8 May. Soon after delivery, she and her sisterships worked on the GLE Lines service linking London and Amsterdam to ports on the Great Lakes. Renamed *Arfell* in 1987, she reverted to *Jan* in January 1991. Later in the year she was sold to Irish owners and renamed *Bell Swift*. We see her at Avonmouth on 6 December 1993. On completion of her Bell Lines work in autumn 1997, she was renamed *Swift* and on 22 September 1997 she left Antwerp for Port Everglades to trade from there to various Caribbean ports. She returned to Antwerp from Port Everglades and Miami on 15 February 2000. In 2002 she was sold to Norwegian owners, renamed *Line*, and converted to a self-discharger fitted with a Caterpillar excavator. She was recycled at Grenå in late June 2011.

(Bernard McCall)

There were just two examples of the 83d design. Although they had a 250 TEU capacity compared to the 195 TEU of the basic Type 83, unlike other ships in the series they were not built as container ships but were ordered by Herman Wulff to carry cellulose on charter to Södra. For this purpose they were equipped with two 15-tonne Hagglund cranes. Launched on 16 April 1978, *Hildegard Wulff* was delivered on 22 May. She was renamed *Cellus* in 1983 and became *Flora* following a sale in 1998. At this point her cranes were removed and she traded henceforth as a container ship. She left northern Europe in 2003 and started to trade in the Mediterranean as *Yamak 3*. She became *Geza Hope* in 2004 and *Sarah Star* in 2008, being eventually recycled at Aliaga in February 2012.

(Bernard McCall collection)

The final two ships of the second batch for Morocco were designated Type 83e, the final one being **Oualidia** which was launched on 9 October 1978 and delivered on 25 November. Typical voyages would see her trading from Casablanca and Agadir to ports in Europe such as Bilbao, Le Havre, Southampton and Antwerp. She was photographed on the New Waterway on 14 June 1984. She was laid up at Caen in late December 2001 and in September 2002 she was sold to owners in Cambodia and renamed **Ilania Star**. She then traded mainly between Vlissingen and St Petersburg. She became **Amer-F** in April 2007 following a further sale and henceforth traded in the eastern Mediterranean and Black Sea. She was recycled at Aliaga in August 2011.

(David Gallichan, Bernard McCall collection)

As noted on page 1, all three of the Type 87 ferries had interesting histories. The **Buffalo** was the second of the trio that had been ordered by Stena Line. She was laid down as **Stena Traveller** but prior to delivery was chartered to P&O for the Irish Sea services then being introduced. She was launched as **Buffalo** on 6 January 1975 and delivered on 26 March to Hain-Nourse Ltd, part of the P&O Group. She and sistership **Bison** entered service on the Pandoro service between Fleetwood and Larne. We see her leaving Fleetwood on 27 July 1987. In 1988 she was lengthened at the Hall, Russell shipyard in Aberdeen and again at A&P in Falmouth ten years later. She was then renamed **European Leader**, becoming **Stena Leader** in 2004. The Fleetwood route was closed in 2010 and after a lay-up in Belfast, all three ferries were sold to Russian owners, **Buffalo** being renamed **Anna Marine**. Initially trading between Zonguldak (Turkey) and Skadowsk (Ukraine), **Anna Marine** was selected to open a trial service from April 2012, initially between Mersin (Turkey) and Port Said (Egypt) and from there through the Suez Canal to Duba (Saudi Arabia) from June. The service was abandoned after three months. Her final months were just like those of **Stena Seafarer**.

(Bernard McCall)

In the mid-1970s, several shipyards in northern Europe revived the idea of building sea-going ships that could sail inland on rivers and canals. It was felt that this would reduce the need for transhipment of cargoes. A common feature of these ships was their low air draught which was achieved by building them with either a very low superstructure or a wheelhouse that could be raised and lowered hydraulically. The first Sietas design of this kind was the Type 88 five of which were built between 1976 and 1979. The second example was *Ostemaat*, launched on 15 April 1976 and delivered on 11 May. We see her in Alexandra Dock, Hull, soon after delivery. She was arrested and laid up in Rotterdam on 3 March 1986, and was sold in mid-June being renamed *Lai da Toma*. A sale in 1994 saw her renamed *Mari Galante* and then *Lagik* in 1996. Her end came after she grounded and broke her back while swinging in the River Nene at Sutton Bridge on 13 December 2000. She blocked the river for 44 days and was broken up in situ.

(Bernard McCall)

The first three examples of Type 88 were followed by two of Type 88a which were modified and had a slightly higher deadweight. The **Jork** was the first of this pair. Launched on 13 January 1978, she was delivered as **Pirat** on 15 February. She was renamed **Hip Pancevo** in 1981 and reverted to **Pirat** two years later. She remained in German ownership throughout her career, taking the names **Solveig** (1987), **Ortrud** (1991), **Runner** (2001) and **Jork** (2006). She was photographed at Breiholz on the Kiel Canal on 30 June 2007. Only five weeks later, on 4 August 2007 she collided with the unmanned gas platform Viking Echo in the North Sea while on passage from Lübeck to New Holland. Her crew of six was rescued before the ship sank. Her Polish master was later sentenced to a year in gaol for being three times over the legal limit for alcohol.

(Koos Goudriaan)

The two Type 89 ships were larger than any previous vessels built at the Sietas yard. With a length of over 150 metres, they had tonnages of 8084grt and 11031dwt. Both were built for Jugoslavenska Plovidba, of Rijeka which was in the former Yugoslavia. The *Susak* was the first to be delivered, this being on 28 January 1977. Both ships were sold in 1991, the *Susak* being acquired by owners in Malta but she was not renamed until bought by a London-based company in 2002 when she became *Claudia A*. Sold to Greek owners she became *Rialto* two years later and was recycled at Alang in 2009. She was photographed as she passed Kandilli on the Asian side of the Bosphorus on 1 June 2008.

(Simon Smith)

12

The only Type 90 vessel was a ro/ro built for a ten-year time charter to Poseidon Shipping. Launched on 27 August 1976, she was delivered as *Transgermania* on 30 October. On 27 December 1990 she suffered grounding damage when 50 miles off Turku during a voyage from Hull to Helsinki. She was repaired in Turku and returned to service on 24 June 1991. Sold in 1993, she was renamed *Rosebay*, later becoming *Eurostar* and *Eurocruiser* (1997), *Rosebay* again (1998), *Transparaden* (2001) and *Translandia* (2004). She was recycled at Alang in late May 2014. Our photograph shows her at the Hook of Holland in July 1984 when she was on charter to Stena Line and trading between Harwich and the Hook. As *Eurostar* she worked on Sally Line's service between Ramsgate and Ostend; as *Transparaden* she connected Riga and Lübeck, also Klaipeda and Fredericia, and as *Translandia* she worked between Helsinki and Tallinn for Eckero Line.

(Bernard McCall)

The five examples of Type 92 were certainly unusual. The first four were built in 1977 and were subcontracted to the Blohm & Voss shipyard in Hamburg. They were multipurpose ro/ro lo/lo ships with a container capacity of 219TEU. The third example was launched on 2 September 1977 and delivered as *Osteexpress* on 20 October. In the following year she was renamed *Ghazi II* for a charter and further charters saw her become *Zim Caribe* in 1979 and *Elma Ocho* in 1981 before returning to *Osteexpress* in 1982. A further charter in 1986 saw her renamed *Scandutch Iberia*, later becoming *North Empress* in 1987, *Dutch Liner* in 2000, *Fort Ross* in 2004 and *Fusion* in 2010. She was last reported at Puerto Montt in Chile in mid-2019.

(Koos Goudriaan collection)

The *North King* was not built until 1988 and was constructed at the Sietas yard. Her superstructure differed from that of the earlier vessels and she was denoted as Type 92a. She was delivered as *North King* on 1 March 1988. All ships of the type were popular with charterers and their frequent renaming reflects this. The *North King* has had comparatively few names, becoming *Dutch Runner* in 2000, *P&O Nedlloyd Douala* in 2001 and reverting to *Dutch Runner* in 2002. Although all the class have traded worldwide, they have spent much time in Canada and in 2008 this vessel came into the ownership of Great Lakes Feeder Lines. On at least two occasions she was laid up in Canadian ports. More recently she has been trading in the Caribbean, being a regular visitor to Port au Prince in Haiti and last reported there in July 2020. The photograph of *North King* was taken at Port Everglades on 28 March 1996.

(Oliver Sesemann)

The three Type 93 ships were all container vessels with a 428TEU capacity and the second to be delivered was **Westermühlen**, launched on 22 May 1978 and delivered on 29 June. She was taken on charter by Zim Israel and renamed **Zim Eilat** in 1979 and **Zim Export** in 1982 before reverting to her original name the following year. In fact, all three ships were chartered by Zim Israel and by Gracechurch Borchard Lines. It was in 1983 that this vessel was chartered briefly by the latter company and renamed **Miriam Borchard** before reverting to **Westermühlen** later in the year and becoming **Miriam Borchard** again in 1985. We see her passing Rozenburg on the New Waterway on 3 July 1985. Her end came on 8 March 1988 when she sank after colliding with another vessel while on passage from Limassol to London.

(David Gallichan, Bernard McCall collection)

Very much a one-off in the Type 94 series was **Westermoor**, launched on 3 June 1977 and delivered on 29 June. She differed from the other ships in being fitted with two 35-tonne cranes. She was renamed **Essex Courage** in 1983 and on 19 May 1983 she left the River Tees at the start of a voyage to Vigo and Ascension. She returned to the River Tees on 8 July and reverted to **Westermoor**. She was photographed on the New Waterway on 9 May 1984. Sold in 1986, she became **West Moor** and in 1995 she was taken on charter by Zim Israel and traded between Fos, Barcelona and Valencia as **Zim Espana**. She was renamed **Harmony** following a sale in 2001 and became **Mansour M** in 2009. She traded in the eastern Mediterranean and Middle East until sold for recycling at Alang in January 2017.

(David Gallichan, Bernard McCall collection)

There is some confusion about the various Type 94 ships. The four basic Type 94 vessels were less than 100 metres in length and had a 306TEU capacity. One of these was **Peter Knüppel**, launched on 17 October 1977 and delivered to Hans Herman Knüppel on 15 November. She was popular with major charterers as evidenced by her names. She was **Eurobridge Link** (1978 – 1980), **Katherine Borchard** (1982 – 1983), **City of Salerno** (1984 – 1986), **Maersk Tempo** (1987 – 1991), **Zim Black Sea** (2000 – 2001).

On each occasion she returned briefly to her original name before the next charter started. In 2001 she was sold to Norwegian owners and became **Liv**. We see her at Felixstowe on 31 May 1989 when she was shuttling between the East Anglian port and Europoort as **Maersk Tempo**. She was recycled at Grenå in Denmark as **Liv** during November 2011.

(Bernard McCall)

The two Type 94a ships had a 319TEU capacity, were six metres longer than the Type 94 and also were fitted with two 35-tonne cranes. This example was launched as **Hansedamm** on 10 December 1978 but delivered as **Karaman** on 31 December. Renamed **Ville du Zenith** for a charter on 30 January 1985, she reverted to **Hansedamm** on 8 May 1985. Further charters saw her become **Scandutch Sicilia** on 18 December 1986 and **Nedlloyd Antilles** on 16 January 1992. Sold in January 1996, she became

Dania Suhr two years later. Further charters saw her renamed **MSC Ecuador** in October 2001, **Sea Tiger** in July 2002 and **Eco Yasmin** in March 2004. In December 2004 she was sold to Norwegian operators and renamed **Heidi**. Her two cranes were removed and she was fitted with an 85-tonne Hitachi excavator to equip her for trade in the Baltic and Scandinavia as a self-discharger. We see her at Moldefjorden on 20 June 2012.

(Charlie McCurdy)

The two Type 94b ships were five metres longer than the Type 94a and again had two 35-tonne cranes. The ship seen here was launched as **Ostebay** on 28 February 1979 and delivered as **Kalymnos** on 6 April. She reverted to **Ostebay** in 1981 and three years later was taken on long-term time charter to the Iceland Steamship Company and renamed **Skogafoss**. In December 1990 the ship was acquired by her charterers. She became **Maersk Georgetown** for a charter in late July 1998 and reverted to **Skogafoss** in April 1999 before being sold to Malaysian owners by whom she was renamed **Bougainvilla**. A subsequent sale in 2008 saw her renamed **Ocean Carrier** and she was photographed as such at anchor off Singapore on 21 June 2009. Finally she was renamed **Mujur 3** in 2012 before being recycled in China in December of that year.

(Krispen Atkinson)

A total of 26 examples of Type 95 were built between 1977 and 1980 and they comprised five different sub-types. The basic design comprised sixteen ships each of which had a 127TEU container capacity with 53TEU in the hold and 74TEU on deck. An example of the basic design was *Britta*, launched on 11 June 1977 and delivered on 30 June. Within a month of delivery she was chartered by United States Lines and renamed

American Cheyenne as seen here passing the Hook of Holland on 2 June 1978. On completion of the charter in 1979 she was renamed *Britta I* and then *Britta II* in 1987. In May 1992 she was converted to a tanker for the carriage of liquid carbon dioxide and was renamed *Hydrogas II*, becoming *Yara Gas II* in 2004. She was recycled at Frederikshavn in 2013.

(Bernard McCall)

At least five of the Type 95 vessels have been converted for different purposes, two of them becoming tankers for the carriage of liquefied carbon dioxide. With the Neuenfelde yard at full capacity, construction of **Este** was subcontracted to the Norderwerft shipyard in Hamburg. She was launched on 25 November 1977 and delivered to Paul & Ernst August Rüsch on 22 December. She was sold in late 1988 and on 3 January 1989 arrived at Santander from Hamburg to be converted for her new role as **Hydrogas** for Norsk Hydro. She returned to trade in April 1989. In 2004, Hydro Agri demerged from Norsk Hydro and took the name Yara International. At the same time their ships were renamed and **Hydrogas** became **Yara Gas I**. She was ultimately recycled at Frederikshavn in April 2013. The photograph was taken at Fredericia on 29 May 1998.

(Bernard McCall)

At least two of the Type 95 ships were eventually sold to Chinese operators. The *Chang Shun Da 18* has become a mystery as her name is not recorded in any European sources and one must go to the Shanghai Marine Safety Agency to identify her. She was launched as *Niedermehnen* on 28 June 1977 but delivered as *Ibesca Portugal* to Osterwisch & Sohn on 26 July. On completion of the charter in 1982 she reverted to *Niedermehnen*. In March 1983 she was arrested in Rotterdam and was sold in the following month to Jürgen Breuer by whom she was renamed *Lady Juliane*, but charters saw her renamed *Akak Victory* in 1984 and *Victory* in 1985 before becoming *Juliane* once again in 1986. In July 1988 she was once again arrested in Rotterdam and was sold in late August to owners in Hong Kong. Named *Fareast Victor*, she left Antwerp at the start of a voyage to Xingang on 7 October 1988. She was sold and renamed *Tong An* in 1989 but there is no date available for when she became *Chang Shun Da 18*. She was photographed at Shanghai on 15 April 2009.

(Simon Smith)

The various Type 95 ships have proved to be ideal for conversion for other uses. The **Trabant**, one of the six Type 95a ships, was launched for Hermann Meyer on 1 July 1978 but delivered to Peter Döhle on 2 August. Much of her early career was spent on charter to Aros Line. In January 1991 she was renamed **Mara** and two years later became **Pentland** to work on the Macvan service linking Rotterdam and Antwerp to Grangemouth and Felixstowe. She was sold to Finnish owners in 1995, being renamed **Anne**, and then **Mari** in 1997 after a sale within Finland. She was fitted with an excavator and used mainly to carry rock armour to other vessels owned by the same company which deposited the cargo offshore. She is seen in Southampton Water on 19 March 2007. After arrival at Le Havre in 2010, she was detained and was eventually sold to owners in Romania. Her excavator was removed and, renamed **Sherin**, worked in the container trades in the Mediterranean and Black Sea. She became **Scorpion I** in 2012, **Shark** in 2017 and **Jaguar** in January 2019.

(Phil Kempsey)

The depth of the hold of the two Type 95b ships is 80 centimetres lower than that of the basic Type 95 and this was partly offset by a higher hatch coaming. The ships were fitted with a modified deckhouse to save weight. They were built for Vega Reederei Friedrich Dauber, the second one being **Tafelberg** which was launched on 10 December 1977 – the same day that sistership **Kiekeberg** was handed over. The pair were built as minibulkers and without a defined container capacity. They were fitted with a modified deckhouse to save weight. In April 1989 both were sold to Poolship, based in the Swedish port of Gävle, and were used mainly in the timber trades from Sweden. The **Tafelberg** was renamed **Nordtrader**. Fitted with a new engine in 1992, she was photographed on the New Waterway near Maassluis on 17 April 2007. She was sold to another Swedish company, Lupin Shipping, in 2009 and was renamed **Lunden** but within a few months was sold to trade under the flag of Georgia as **Armony**. Since 2011 she has been under the Tanzanian flag and is still trading in the eastern Mediterranean and Black Sea.

(Ron Wood)

The **Melton Challenger** was launched on 16 June 1980 and delivered to British owners Melton Securities Ltd on 24 July. The only example of Type 95c, she was built for the carriage of timber. The dimensions of sub-type 95c are identical to those of sub-type 95a. However, the ship had a higher hatch coaming which enabled a greater volume of grain to be carried. As may be expected from the legend on her hull, she spent some time on charter to Cantimber and imported timber from ports on the Great Lakes usually to New Holland on the Humber. She also visited ports such as New York and Baltimore in the USA. We see her in the River Mersey on 21 September 1981. In September 1988 she arrived at Rotterdam for repairs and was sold to Bror Husell of Mariehamn by whom she was renamed **Allgard**. In the following year she was acquired by Dutch owners and renamed **Libra**. A sale to Latvian owners in 2003 saw her become **Skulte** and three years later she was bought by owners in the Faroe Islands and renamed **Atlantic**. In 2012 she was rebuilt as a self-discharger and fitted with an excavator to work in the aggregates trade. She continues to trade as such but in the Caribbean.

(David Gallichan, Bernard McCall collection)

Launched on 23 May 1980 and delivered to Hamburg-based Peter Ebeling on 28 June, the only Type 95d coaster was initially named *Frey* and was significant inasmuch as she was subcontracted to the Norderwerft shipyard and was the final newbuilding at this yard. The sub-type 95d, designed as a multipurpose cargo ship, was based on the sub-type 95b but was fitted with reinforced hatch covers so that two layers of containers could be stowed on deck. On entering service she worked on the Rheintainer-Linie service of RMS, linking Rhine ports and Rotterdam mainly to ports in the UK and Ireland. She was renamed *Hunte* following a sale within Germany in 1990.

In late 1991 she sailed to New Zealand and traded between there and Australia for a time and then extensively between Auckland and other ports, not returning to Europe until late 1996. On 28 December 2001 she grounded on the island of Texel and was subsequently laid up at Ridderkerk. In early 2003 she was sold to Syrian owners and renamed *Hunter*, becoming *Nasip* in 2007. She was recycled at Aliaga in September 2017. She was photographed on 3 July 2016 at Haydarpaşa in the Asian part of Istanbul.

(Simon Smith)

26

Tthe basic Type 96 had a 208TEU capacity and ffive examples of the design were built, the **Nordsee** being one of these. Subcontracted to the Norderwerft shipyard, she was launched on 26 May 1978 and was delivered to Rendsburg-based Walter Jess on 30 June. In summer 1996 she was chartered by Seaboard and left Dublin for Miami on 13 July. Soon renamed **Seaboard Clipper**, she then traded from Miami to Barbados, Port au Prince and other Caribbean ports. She left Miami for Port au Prince for the final time on 15 January 1999 and then crossed the Atlantic arriving in Dublin on 29 January. She sailed on to Antwerp where the charter was completed and she reverted to **Nordsee** on 12 February. We see her in the River Mersey on 4 December 2006 heading for Greenock from the container terminal at Irlam on the Manchester Ship Canal. In 2008 she was sold to Greek operators and renamed **Efstratios**, thus ending a 30-year period in the ownership of the Jess family. She arrived in Volos on 23 July 2008 and commenced trading in the Mediterranean in 2009. She was recycled at Aliaga in late December 2016.

(David Williams)

The two Type 96a ships were built for Friedrich Beutelrock, of Lübeck, and saw this company return to shipowning after selling four ro/ro vessels in 1974. They differed from the basic Type 96 in having extra ventilation in the hold and they had ten connections on deck for refrigerated containers. Both were built for the owner's Continent – Israel service as indicated by the letters on the ship's hull. The **Thunar** was launched on 21 February 1979, her forepart having been built at the Sietas yard and taken to the Norderwerft yard where the aft section had been built. In December 1982 she went to the Remontowa shipyard in Szczecin where she was lengthened by 14.46 metres, increasing her container capacity from 208TEU to 247TEU. She went on to work in various parts of the world under different names, becoming **Prime View** (1993), **Alcyon** (2000), **Mathish** (2001), **Sar Mathish** (2002), **Ghazee** (2003), **Aljazy Hope** (2005) and finally **Almostafa** (2007). She was recycled at Aliaga in March 2014.

(David Gallichan, Bernard McCall collection)

The solitary Type 96b ship was **Hornbaltic** and she differed from the others in being fitted with a 14-tonne crane. She was launched on 10 February 1980 and delivered to Horn-Linie as **Hornbelt** on 12 March. She became **Hornbaltic** on 28 May 1980 and was renamed **Adils** for a charter on 6 October 1993. She reverted to **Hornbaltic** on 9 May 1994 and for the next six years passed through various subsidiaries of Horn-Linie. We see her at Hamburg on 18 May 1996. Sold out of the fleet in August 2000, she was renamed **Rhapsody** and became **Hesen Moon** in 2009. In 2016 she was bought by Lebanese owners, renamed **Talia** and converted to a livestock carrier. She remains busy throughout the Mediterranean in 2021.

(Oliver Sesemann)

29

Only two examples of Type 96c were built, the first being *Clipper* which was launched on 23 April 1980 and delivered to Harald Winter on 29 May as *Manchester Clipper* for charter to Manchester Liners. On completion of the charter in July 1983, she reverted to *Clipper* and was sold to another Hamburg owner, Rolf Fischer, in June 1991. Chartered once again in October 1991, she was renamed *ECL Cadet*, reverting to *Jupiter* briefly in late April 1992 before being taken on charter by K-Line and renamed *Iberian Bridge* on 18 May 1992. Later sales/charters saw her become *Borstel* in 1993 and *Paaschburg* in 1996. On 5 August 2003, she was seen on the Kiel Canal heading for Gothenburg from Hamburg. On 7 May 2008 she arrived at Emden and eventually left on 18 July, named *Lady Marah* and heading for the Mediterranean via Pasajes. In June 2010 she was sold and renamed *FGM Istanbul*, becoming *Pendik* in 2011 and *My Violet* in 2013. She was still trading in the eastern Mediterranean in 2021.

(Bernard McCall)

The only Type 97 ship was the cement carrier *Sunnanvik* which was launched on 9 July 1978 and delivered in September of that year. She has passed through the hands of several Swedish owners in her career and remains at work over 40 years after being delivered. On 29 June 2015 she grounded off Holmsund in the north of the Gulf of Bothnia because of a steering failure. She was refloated the next day with damage to her ballast tanks but not to her cargo spaces. She was repaired and remains in service. We see her battling through the ice near Luleå in northern Sweden on 10 April 2016.

(Igor Dilo)

The only Type 98 ship was a cement carrier. She was launched on 23 November 1977 and delivered as *Elbia* on 19 January 1978. When she entered service, she was working in the Indian Ocean and visiting locations such as Mombasa, Mauritius, Colombo and the Seychelles. By the mid-1980s she was trading on the east coast of the USA and from the start of the new millenium she was back in the Indian Ocean, then in the Caribbean and later in the Mediterranean. We see her anchored off Piraeus on 29 August 2008. She retained the same name throughout her career and was recycled at Alang in May 2011.

(Peter Fitzpatrick)

There were two Type 99 ships and these were also cement carriers, the first to be delivered being **Gloria Elena** which was launched on 4 May 1981 and delivered on 15 July. They were slightly larger than **Elbia**. Both were built for trading from ports in Mexico and early in her career **Gloria Elena** worked between Mexico and US ports such as Houston, Jacksonville and Port Everglades. In more recent years she has traded mainly along the Mexican coast visiting ports such as Tampico and Coatzacoalcos. She was photographed at the latter port on 19 March 2012. She remains hard at work in 2021.

(Captain Theo Hinrichs)

Only two ships of Type 100 were delivered, the first being **Conti Belgica** which was launched on 18 March 1978 and delivered on 29 April. Both were fitted with two 6-tonne and two 50-tonne cranes. She was only six weeks old when photographed leaving Heysham on 16 June 1978. In 1980 she was renamed **Blue Bell** and **Martinique**, then **Ville D'Aurore** in 1981, all for brief charters, and reverted to **Conti Belgica** in 1982. On 8 July 1987 she foundered off the coast of Oman when on passage from Batangas to Sweden. Her crew of fifteen was rescued by two lifeboats from a nearby gas tanker.

Contimar Linienagentur was established in 1974 on behalf of a carrier handling break bulk cargo to the eastern Mediterranean. With the world economy changing rapidly in the early 1980s the company changed its focus from being a pure liner agency to become an independent ship broker for worldwide break bulk cargo. The company was renamed COLI Schiffahrt & Transport, keeping the initials "CO" and "LI" of its former name.

(Bernard McCall)

Three ships of Type 100a were built in 1983/84, the last one being **Conti Holandia** which was delivered on 21 March 1984 They differed from the original two ships in having only two 50-tonne cranes and had less powerful engines. All three were transferred in 1987 to the newly-formed subsidiary company CPC Consolidated Pool Carriers and this ship was renamed **CPC Holandia**. In 1996 she was sold to Danish owners and renamed **Stevns Pearl**, becoming **Diana Scan** between December 2005 and October 2009 for a time charter to Scan-Trans Shipping. On completion of the charter she was renamed **Stevns Pearl** and retained this name until sold in 2012, becoming **Yamak Junior**. She was recycled at Alang in 2017. She was photographed in the New Waterway on 2 May 1986.

(David Gallichan, Bernard McCall collection)

The late 1970s saw an increased demand for larger container feeder ships and the three Type 101 vessels reflected this. They were gearless and had a 462TEU capacity. The first was launched on 31 May 1979 and delivered as *Concordia* to Gerd Koppelmann on 20 July. She was soon taken on charter by Zim Israel and renamed *Zim Australia*. She reverted to *Concordia* in 1982 and was then chartered twice by Borchard Lines becoming *Katherine Borchard* on 20 September 1985 until 14 February 1986 and starting the next one on 16 July 1986. Her next change of name was in 2000 when she became *Dania-Carina* following a sale to Uwe Suhr. She left German ownership in 2007 having been acquired by Norwegian owners and renamed *Tone*. She was recycled at Klaipeda in May 2014.

(David Gallichan, Bernard McCall collection)

The two basic Type 102 ships had a 411TEU capacity and were fitted with two 35-tonne cranes, making them ideal for feeder container trades in areas where shore-based cargo handling facilities were less than ideal. This ship was launched on 8 September 1980 and delivered as *Estetrader* on 10 October. For the first fifteen years of her career, she had a series of names thanks to frequent charters. She became *Auvergne* (1982), *Esteclipper* and then *Kahira* (1983) and *Kalkara* (1984) for a charter to Deutschen Nah-Ost Linien (DNOL), *Estetrader* (1986), *City of Athens* (1987), and *Emstrader* and *Sea Trader* (1991). Sold for trade in the Far East in 1996, she was renamed *Tiger Sea* and then *Gilian*. In 2005 she was renamed *Bahar Mas* when sold to Indonesian owners and continues to trade in Indonesian waters. The *Kalkara* was photographed on the New Waterway on 17 April 1985.

(David Gallichan, Bernard McCall collection)

The only Type 102a ship was launched as *Altona* on 4 November 1980 and delivered as *Karyatein* to Hamburg-based Dieter Behrens on 12 December. She also had two 35-tonne cranes but had a 436TEU container capacity. She was photographed in the New Waterway on 26 September 1983 when inward bound from Alexandria. In early February 1989 she went on charter to Manchester Liners as *Manchester Trader,* reverting to *Altona* on 3 June 1991. The next charter saw her become *Nedlloyd Lotus* in February 1993, returning to her original name two years later. Between 2005 and 2007 she was chartered as *Mekong Valiance* and was eventually sold in 2010 to be renamed *Letfallah V* by her new Syrian owners. She was recycled at Alang in early 2014.

(David Gallichan, Bernard McCall collection)

The only Type 102c ship had a slightly larger container capacity of 445TEU. She was launched as **Alcyone** on 17 July 1982 for well-known Bremen-based owner Argo Reederei Richard Adler & Söhne. She was delivered on 25 September as **Kastamonu** for charter by Deutschen Nah-Ost Linien. In mid-1985, she was briefly renamed **Contship Lugano** for a sub-let before reverting to **Kastamonu**. At the end of her charter in 1988, she was again renamed **Alcyone**. She is seen arriving at La Spezia on 16 September 1992. Sold in December 1992, she was renamed **Dania** and a charter saw her become **Nedlloyd Daisy** for a few months in 1993. A sale to Spanish owners saw her become **Maersk Canarias** in November 1994. Sold to In 1999 she was acquired by Peter Döhle and renamed **Jan D**. She left northern Europe in 2011 following a sale and renaming to **Span Asia I**, this becoming simply **Asia I** for her voyage to breakers at Chattogram in December 2020.

(Carlo Martinelli)

In the early 1980s, the Sietas yard decided to enter the chemical tanker market and this resulted in Type 103. The **Multitank Arcadia** was the first of four tankers built for Hamburg-based Christian Ahrenkiel. She was launched on 25 November 1980 and delivered on 6 February 1981. She is seen in the New Waterway on 18 May 1984 heading from Rotterdam to Antwerp. In late 1985 she and her sisters were lengthened by ten metres. At the time, this group of tankers was highly regarded in the industry. Among their contracts was one to deliver acrylonitrile from Seal Sands on the River Tees to various ports in Spain, Italy and Turkey. She was sold to Turkish operators in 1998 and renamed **Chem Princess**. By 2007 she was trading exclusively in the eastern Mediterranean and Black Sea and she was recycled at Alang in January 2008.

(David Gallichan, Bernard McCall collection)

With Type 104, we are faced with some problems. There are five different primary sources of information and they fail to agree on which vessels should be placed in each of the sub-groups. There is agreement, however, that only two ships exemplified the basic Type 104. One of these was *Condor*, the first of the Type 104 ships to be completed. Launched on 21 November 1978, she was delivered to owner Paul Häse, of Stade, on 20 December. She was a special vessel in that she was fitted with two stainless steel tanks for the carriage of china clay slurry, one forward and one aft with a conventional hold midships. She was one of seven ships thus fitted, five of them being built at the Sietas shipyard. The intention was that they should carry slurry from the UK and return with cargoes usually of steel. The basic Type 104 ships had an overall length of 73.09 metres. The *Condor* was photographed in April 1990 as she exchanged pilots on the River Seine on her way to St Etienne-du-Rouvray, upstream of Rouen, where she discharged at a large paper mill. In 1998 she was sold and converted to an edible oil tanker named *Bernice*. She became *Nani* in 2008 and was recycled at Aliaga in 2010.

(Bernard McCall)

There are four vessels that can be identified with certainty as Type 104a with an overall length of 85.83 metres. One of these was launched on 19 December 1979 and delivered as *Jan* to Hamburg-based Jürgen Stahmer on 29 December. In 1987 she was sold to Belgian owners and in summer of that year she was converted in Antwerp to a chemical tanker named *Gent*. In 2001 she was renamed *Eva-H*, then *Maria* in 2003 followed by *Britt* in 2005 and *Sea Light* in 2017. We see her arriving at Aberdeen on 30 December 2006. She was last reported at Cristobal near the entrance to the Panama Canal in May 2020, possibly working as a bunkering tanker. Dominating the background is the port's VTS centre while the former VTS centre is the building to the left of the photograph.

(David Dodds)

Much comparing of notes leads us to the conclusion that there are three Type 104b ships and these are 7.86 metres longer than the basic design. All of them were fitted with tanks for the carriage of china clay slurry. The *Pandor* was launched on 5 March 1980 and delivered to Paul Häse on 3 April. The *Condor* had inaugurated the china clay slurry exports in 1979 with deliveries to the Haindl paper mill at Walsum near Duisburg on the River Rhine. The entry into service of *Pandor* enabled a wider range of mills to be served. She was photographed as she arrived at Fowey from Swansea on 4 August 1981. Sold in 1997, she was renamed *Wiebke D* and her tanks were removed. In 2018 she was sold within Germany and renamed *Stefanie F* under the flag of Panama. She continues to trade in northern Europe.

(Bernard McCall)

Having been launched on 2 July 1980, the solitary Type 104d vessel was delivered to Klaus Jürgens as **Birgit Jürgens** on 13 September 1980. In 1988 she was sold to Portuguese owners and renamed **Almar**. On 31 December 1997 she was laid up at Slikkerveer and then arrested in early September 1999. She was later sold and converted to a vegetable oil tanker, eventually leaving Rotterdam on 23 February 2000. We see her on the New Waterway on 22 December 2008. She arrived at 's Gravendeel on 20 May 2009 and was laid up once again. She was sold to owners in the Middle East in mid-2010 and left Dordrecht on 24 June heading for Port Said and then Colombo. By September of the following year she had been renamed **Fateh 1**. She was eventually recycled at Alang in 2019.

(Koos Goudriaan)

The two Type 105 ships were built for Hermann Wulff of Kollmar to be chartered to Aros Lines for their service from Sweden mainly carrying packaged timber to the UK, especially the ports of Goole and Lowestoft. The first to be completed was **Lady Bos** which was launched on 12 June 1979 and delivered on 17 July. She was photographed as she left Sunderland on 20 March 1982 during a visit by Yorkshire Ship Enthusiasts. In 1990 she transferred to the Swedish flag and then passed through the hands of several owners. In January 2002 she was renamed **Norrvik** having been taken on time charter by Jönsson Nova, a Swedish logistics company. In 2017 she was sold to a Greek owner, renamed **Taxiarchis** and fitted with an excavator. She continues to trade around the Greek islands.

(Bernard McCall)

The two Type 105a ships were designed as container feeder ships. The second of the type was *Craigantlet*, launched as *Neptunus* on 18 April 1983 but delivered as *Craigantlet* on 16 June. The name is a link back to a previous ship owned by Hugh Craig & Co, Belfast coal merchants and shipowners established in 1842, and to two subsequent ships chartered from German owners. On entering service, she and sistership *Craigavad* (another long-established Craig name) which had been launched as *Saturnus* traded between Garston and Belfast. She reverted to *Neptunus* in 1988 and remained in German ownership in 1995 when she was renamed *Pellworm*, linking Cardiff to Dublin (and occasionally Belfast)

for Cardiff Container Line. In 1998 she was renamed *Coastal Wave* for the Coastal Container Line service between Liverpool and Belfast. By the date of this photograph, 10 June 2005, she was also serving Dublin. There was a change of area in 2009 when she was sold and renamed *Huelin Endeavour* for a service linking Portsmouth (and later Southampton) to the Channel Islands. In 2013 she was sold and converted to a livestock carrier named *Jaohar Discovery* and then *Karazi*. She continues to trade in the Middle East under the Sierra Leone flag.

(Mike Hemming)

Rather surprisingly there was only one Type 107 ship to be built and this was **Vera Rambow**, launched on 12 February 1979 and delivered to Helmuth and Wilfried Rambow on 10 March. Managed by Wagenborg, she came into the ownership of this Dutch company as **Waalborg** in 1989. Four years later she was sold to Cypriot owners but remained in Wagenborg management as **Hydra** until sold and renamed **Elm** in 2000.

Acquired by Polish owners in 2002 she was renamed **Rega** and then moved to Turkish owners in 2010 initially without a change of name until 2018 when she became **Neva**. She has since been sold for recycling at Aliaga where she was beached on 27 April 2021. We see her as **Hydra** heading west on the Kiel Canal on passage from Kalmar to Ipswich on 21 July 1995.

(Bernard McCall)

The solitary Type 108 ship was not built at the Sietas yard, nor in fact at any shipyard in Germany. She was a product of the Georgi Dimitrov yard in Varna. She was a conventional bulk carrier, launched as **Helvetia** on 12 August 1980 and delivered on 17 December. After trading for almost one year she arrived in Hamburg on 2 November 1981 for conversion to a cement carrier, eventually leaving on 28 January 1982 for Barcelona. She was photographed at this Spanish port in August 1996. Detained at Port Louis, Mauritius, in late 2006, she returned to trade in July 2007 but she was sold for recycling in India in December 2008.

(Lee Brown)

The chance of seeing any commercial ship in the Cumberland Basin in Bristol in 1992 was very remote. To see two was astonishingly unusual, and to see two Sietas-built coasters was almost beyond belief. But that certainly happened on 16 March 1992. The arrival of the Type 58 **Sykron** was featured on page 1 of the previous Sietas book and she can be seen on the opposite side of the Basin. Nearest the camera is **Verena**, a Type 109 vessel. Both ships had arrived to load project cargoes for Grangemouth. The **Verena** was launched on 9 January 1981 and delivered as **Ina Lehmann** on 12 February. She became **Verena** in 1989 and later **Sydgard** (1993), **Sydland** (2004), **Sherin** (2012) and **Amira** (2015). Flying the flag of Turkey, she remains busy in the Mediterranean.

(Bernard McCall)

The two ships of Type 109 were built for Hans Lehmann, of Lübeck. The first was **Siegfried Lehmann**, launched on 2 December 1980 and delivered on 30 December. She was the third vessel in the Lehmann fleet to be named thus. We see her at Neath Abbey Wharf on the River Neath on 4 August 2004 when she was discharging coking coal from Szczecin. In late 2011 she was sold and renamed **Juhaynna** under the flag of Togo and in mid-December she left Helsingborg at the start of a voyage to Nea Karvali in Greece. Since that time she has continued to trade in the Mediterranean and Black Sea, no change to her trading pattern being noted after her sale in 2015 when she became **Rayan**.

(Bill Moore)

Fifteen examples of the basic Type110 were built. The second to the eighth in the series were financed in a single package and were nicknamed the "seven girls", all being given girls' names. One of these was *Carola*, launched on 9 November 1981 and delivered to Heinz Georg Vöge, of Hamburg, on 30 December. Sold and renamed *Lania* in 1994, she was acquired later that year by Guido Lührs, of Wischhafen. In 1998 she was bought by the then harbour master at Wischhafen, Dietmar Grothmann, who named her *Andrea* after his wife. We see her arriving at Sharpness on 9 April 2004. Sold within Germany in 2007, she became *Merlin* and four years later left northern Europe to trade in the Mediterranean and Black Sea as *Gulf River*. In 2019 she was bought by a Greek owner and since then, after being fitted with a deck crane, has traded mainly to Greek ports as *Mastrokostas*.

(Bernard McCall)

Of the seven examples of Type 110a, five were built for Vega Reederei Friedrich Dauber. Unlike the basic Type 110 ships, all had a fixed wheelhouse. The **Mühlenberg** was launched on 21 November 1985 and delivered on 9 January 1986. The Vega funnel is evident in this image of **Mühlenberg** outward bound in ballast in the New Waterway on 16 June 1986. She was sold in October 2006 to Charles M Willie & Co (Shipping) Ltd and became **Celtic Mariner** with Cardiff registry. In 2013 she was sold to Turkish operators and renamed **Tahsin Kalkavan**. She continues to be busy in the Mediterranean.

(Roland Whaite, Bernard McCall collection)

The four Type 110b ships were 3.90 metres longer than the basic design. The third of the four to be delivered was *Petra-Gunda*, launched on 7 December 1985 and completed for Hans Heinrich, of Jork. Ten years later she was sold to Hans-August Sabban, of Hamburg, and renamed *Marlies Sabban*. In February 2006 she too was acquired by Charles M Willie & Co (Shipping) Ltd and was renamed *Celtic Freedom*. We see her outward bound in ballast in the River Mersey on 21 April 2012 as she passes the Albert Dock warehouse. Sold to Turkish owners in 2013, she was renamed *Aykop Emice* and became *Muhammet Gumustas 4* in 2015.

(Darren Hillman)

The two Type 110c vessels had a deeper hold than the earlier ships and a wheelhouse that could be raised still further. The first of the pair was **Gerda Rambow**, launched on 29 July 1985 and delivered to Helmuth and Wilfried Rambow on 11 September. As can be seen clearly in this image of her at Montrose at high water on 6 February 1989, she was on charter to Wagenborg and for a large part of her early career she delivered salt from Hengelo in the Netherlands to Stockholm and Umeå in Sweden, returning with timber or paper products. In 1995 she was sold by Rambow to Portuguese owners and renamed **Coimbra** and a decade later became **Ivy** for VW Nyki Shipping. By 2015 she was trading in the Mediterranean and she was renamed **Ivy 1** in 2017.

(Bernard McCall)

Launched on 24 November 1983 and delivered as **Robert** to Heinz Georg Vöge, of Hamburg, on 30 December, this ship was the first of three examples of the basic Type 111 design. Soon after delivery she was renamed **Akak Success** for a charter in January 1984 and then in August 1984 she became **Gracechurch Crown** for a further charter. In 1986 she reverted to her original name of **Robert** and on 22 December 1990 she collided with a Chinese vessel off the German coast and sank. She was raised seven weeks later and after temporary repairs at the Lloyd Werft yard in Bremerhaven she was towed to the Sietas yard for permanent repairs, being lengthened by 14 metres at the same time. A charter saw her become **ECL Commander** in 1991 and then **Robert** again briefly in May 1992 then being renamed **Rhein Partner**. In 1993 she reverted again to **Robert** and her final charter for her German owner saw her renamed **CTE Istanbul** between 2000 and 2001. She left German ownership in 2005 becoming **Apia**, then **Jana** in 2011 and **Nizar** in 2015. We see her under the latter name in the Bosphorus on 26 May 2019.

(David Dixon)

The twelve examples of Type 111a were 4.2 metres longer than the basic type and, more significantly, were fitted with two 30-tonne cranes mounted on the port side. The first to be completed was *Calypso* which was launched on 27 April 1984 and delivered to Hans Heinrich on 8 June. She was one of the first ships to be chartered by the Band Aid charity and became *Band Aid Hope* on 27 November 1985. She reverted to *Calypso* on 21 April 1986 and was renamed *Helga* following a sale within the Heinrich family in autumn 1992. In mid-1993 a charter to Eimskip saw her renamed *Mulafoss* and she reverted to *Helga* on completion of this in 1997. She was sold to Danish owners in October 1998 and renamed *Thor Amalie* and later changes of identity saw her become *Amalie* in 2004, and *Thor Amalie* in 2007. It was in 2008 that she became *Calypso III*. She was photographed at Gibraltar on 26 March 2010. Having been sold and renamed *Tiger 1* in 2010, this proved to be brief as she was wrecked on the breakwater at Tartous, Syria, on 12 December 2010.

(David Dixon)

The solitary example of Type 111b was **Seevetal**. She differed from the basic type in being 8 metres longer and having a deadweight 1000 tonnes greater than the others. She was launched on 17 March 1986 and delivered on 8 May, soon being chartered to Team Lines. In 1998 she was renamed **Pavo** and a subsequent series of charters saw her take several names becoming **Normed Istanbul** (2000), **Pavo** (2001), **Pride of Foynes** and then **Pavo** (2006) until a sale to Norwegian operators saw her become **Ranosen** in 2007. As such we see her at Birkenhead on 6 July 2007. Later she became **Kale** in 2011 and **Reeperbahn** in 2014. She continues to trade in the Baltic and North Sea.

(Darren Hillman)

There were only two Type 112 vessels built. They were multipurpose ro/ro ships with a 325TEU container capacity and a deck-mounted 26-tonne crane. They were built for the South Pacific Forum Line behind which was the Government of the Republic of Tonga and both were managed by the Shipping Corporation of Polynesia. The *Fua Kavenga* was the second of the pair, being launched on 7 October 1979 and delivered on 23 November. In 2002 she was renamed *Capitaine Fern II* and then *Golden Trader* in May 2003. We see her arriving at Napier in New Zealand to load logs for China on 4 June 2006. This was her first voyage following repair after a serious fire at Auckland earlier in the year. She eventually left the flag of Tonga when sold and renamed *Golden Trader 1* in 2006. Managed from Sharjah, she moved to the flag of Panama. She became *Ocean Glory* in 2010 and was recycled at Gadani Beach in December 2011.

(Tony des Landes)

The solitary Type 113 vessel was launched on 30 November 1979 and delivered as **Westerhamm** on 31 December. She had a 542TEU capacity and was equipped with two 35-tonne cranes on her port side. Of all the ships featured in the book, she proved to be the one with most changes of name with nineteen being reported between her delivery and recycling at Aliaga in 2012. She was photographed on the New Waterway inward bound to Rotterdam from Monrovia and Cotonou on 3 May 1985 when named **Nedlloyd Westerhamm**, a name she took in early December 1984 and which she retained only until September 1985. She then had 12 furtherchanges of name, including a return to **Westerhamm** on four occasions following charters, until she became **Algiers Star** in 2005. As such she was recycled at Aliaga in 2012.

(the late John Wiltshire)

With their two 35-tonne cranes and 605TEU container capacity, the eight ships of the Type 114 design were inevitably popular with charterers globally. They were an extended version of the Type 113 and were built between 1981 and 1983. The eighth in the series was *Ursus*, launched as such on 4 March 1983 and delivered as *Aqaba Crown* to Klaus-Wilhelm tom Wörden on 22 April. It would be tedious to list all her names but we should note that amongst others she was chartered by Zim, Delmas, Cie Maritime Belge and Kristian Jebsen. She became *Sestri Star* in 2007 and when photographed at Felixstowe on 4 April 2009 she was on charter to Brointermed Lines, a company based in Harwich and specialising in services to North Africa and the eastern Mediterranean. She was renamed *Lady Massa* in 2015 and was recycled at Alang in February 2020.

(Danny Kelliher jnr)

There were four ships of the Type 115 design. They had a 458TEU container capacity and were fitted with two 35-tonne cranes. The *Ilse Wulff* was the first in the series. She was launched on 26 March 1982 and delivered to Hermann Wulff, of Kollmar, on 22 May. Like similar earlier classes, the ships were popular with charterers especially those using ports with inadequate shore-based equipment. In 1986 she was renamed *Convoy Ranger* and briefly reverted to *Ilse Wulff* in the following year. By the end of 1987 she had been chartered by Borchard Lines as *Rachel Borchard*, returning to her original name in early 1991. By March 1991 she had been sold to owners in Iceland and was renamed *Dettifoss*. She became *Tina* on reverting to German ownership in 2000. We see her arriving in the New Waterway on 6 September 2009. She left northern Europe in 2013 when she was sold to Mediterranean operators and renamed *Rawan*, becoming *Papa Joy* in the following year. She was renamed again in April 2021 and as *Alex S* she continues to trade in the eastern Mediterranean and Black Sea.

(Colin Drayson)

Three Type 116 vessels were built, two of these being built for Bugsier and designated Type 116a but not illustrated here. The *Dorothee* was launched as such on 12 October 1983 but delivered as *Ville du Lumière* on 26 November. She had a container capacity of 800TEU and was fitted with two 35-tonne cranes on her port side. She was recycled at Aliaga in 2012, having had a further seventeen names during her career which included charters to Nedlloyd and to Maersk. We see her passing Rozenburg on the New Waterway on 20 April 1985, inward bound to Rotterdam from Jeddah via Hamburg.

(David Gallichan, Bernard McCall collection)

Seen on the River Elbe inward bound to Hamburg from Haifa via London and Rotterdam on 19 July 1995, the **Levant Neva** was the last of the four Type 117 ships. They were container feeders with a 540TEU capacity and were fitted with two 35-tonne cranes. Another type that was immensely popular with charterers, this example was the last of the four, being launched as **Hansewall** on 17 December 1984 and delivered to Dieter Behrens, of Hamburg, in February 1985 as **Kalymnos** for a charter to Deutschen Nah-Ost-Linie. She became **Miriam Borchard** in 1990 and **Lucy Borchard** in 1992 for charter to Borchard Lines and then **Levant Neva** (1994) and **Levant Lesum** (1996) for charter to Bruno Bischoff. Returning to Borchard Lines, she was renamed **Joanna Borchard** in October 1996 and reverted to **Hansewall** in 1997. Her next charter saw her become **MCC Clipper** in 2005 to trade between Singapore and Port Klang. In 2009 she became **Hansewall** for the final time. Sold in 2013, she was renamed **Span Asia 9** and since then has traded in the Philippines.

(Bernard McCall)

The *Invicta* was a self-discharging cement carrier and was the only example of Type 118. She was launched on 18 March 1983 and left Hamburg on her maiden voyage to Mombasa via Suez on 12 June. In this photograph we see her undergoing trials on the River Elbe. She remained in south-east Asia throughout her career, trading between Réunion, Sri Lanka, Mauritius and Singapore, and she was never renamed. Initially she was managed by Deutsche Afrika-Linien (DAL), a company that had been taken over in 1941 by tanker operator John T Essberger based in Hamburg. By the end of her career she was owned by the Lafarge Group but still managed by Essberger. She was recycled at Aliaga in October 2012. She remained active until her sale for recycling.

(Bernard McCall)

Three Type 119 container feeder ships were built, each with a container capacity of 356TEU. They were very popular with charterers, these including Ellerman, MacAndrews, Commodore Shipping and, as seen here, Feederlink. In fact all three traded for Akak Marine at the start of their careers, this example being the second of the type. She was launched as *Ocean* on 20 September 1983 and renamed *Akak Ocean* in April 1984 before reverting to *Ocean* in 1986. Later in 1986 she was renamed *City of Salerno* then in 1988 *Velazquez* prior to returning to her original name in 1991. She was renamed *Takitimu* in 1994 for a four-year stay in New Zealand and she returned to northern Europe in 1998 to work for Feederlink as *Hajo*, becoming *Clontarf* in 2003. She was photographed as she arrived on the River Tyne on 4 March 2006. Later changes of name saw her become *Antonia B* (2008), *Hassan M* (2018) and *Amany Queen* (2019). In 2021 she continues to trade in the Mediterranean and Adriatic.

(Dominic McCall)

The only Type 120 vessel was launched on 2 July 1983 as **Hans-Günther Bülow** and delivered as **Timbus** to Hermann Wulff on 24 September. Equipped with two 16-tonne cranes, she was a dedicated forest products carrier and was strengthened for the carriage of heavy goods and for navigation in ice. She usually loaded in the Swedish ports of Karlshamn and/or Varberg and often delivered to Genoa in her later years. This photograph of her heading eastwards in the Kiel Canal was taken in March 1999 and in December of that year she was sold to Norwegian owner Mikkal Myklebusthaug and was renamed **Langenes**. Sold in 2014 to owners based in Las Palmas and renamed **Phobos**, she has since traded in the western Mediterranean and to the Iberian peninsula.

(Bernard McCall)

The three Type 121 container ships were a development of the Type 117. They had a capacity of 750TEU and were equipped with two 30-tonne cranes mounted on the port side. Once again they were popular with charterers who included Maersk, Ellerman and Sea-Land. The last of the three to be delivered was *Jan Ritscher*, launched on 28 September 1986 and delivered on 18 November. Ten days after delivery she was renamed *ACT 11*. On completion of this charter she reverted to *Jan Ritscher* on 8 February 1988 but six weeks later was renamed *Independent Pursuit* for a five-year charter to Independent Container Line. During that period she made 60 round trips linking Antwerp and Hamburg to Philadelphia and we see her outward bound in the River Elbe on 1 June 1988. She reverted to *Jan Ritscher* for one month after the ending of this charter and was then sold to Chinese owners by whom she was renamed *Mild Lin*. She was recycled in China in early 2010.

(Bernard McCall)

The five Type 122 vessels were container feeders built for five different German owners but all for charter to Bell Lines. The **Otto Becker**, launched on 26 June 1989, was delivered to Rolf Becker on 28 July. We see her at Avonmouth on 6 December 1993, the first day of Bell Line service at the port following transfer of its Bristol Channel service from Bellport on the River Usk. She had arrived from Rozenburg and was loading for Waterford.

The container crane had been brought by sea from Waterford and had arrived fully assembled on 30 September. Sold within Germany in 2001, she was renamed **Maria Schepers**. In December 2013 she was sold to owners in Uruguay and renamed **Provincias Unidas**. She has not appeared in movement reports since leaving Fray Bentos on 19 January 2021.

(Bernard McCall)

The only Type 124 ship was a tanker built for The Shipping Corporation of Trinidad and Tobago and named *Scott Unity*. She was renamed *NP Unity* in 1995, becoming *S&M Unity* at an unspecified date. The ship was laid up off Port of Spain in March 2006 and was photographed there on 31 May 2010. She is reported to have been sold for recycling locally later in 2010.

(Captain Theo Hinrichs)

The Type 126 ship was not a newbuilding at all but rather a major conversion. Named *Beate*, she was an example of the Neptun-471 design from the Neptun shipyard in Rostock and was acquired by the Thornhope Shipping Company in December 1980 and renamed *Crusader Point*. Her derricks were removed and she was chartered to the Central Electricity Generating Board for six years. On completion of the charter she was laid up at Hartlepool before being sold to German owners. She was then delivered to the Sietas yard where she was lengthened and converted to a liquefied gas tanker named *Olefine Gas*. She was renamed *Chem Olefine* in 1990 and *Norgas Traveller* in 1991. We see her as such outward bound in the Firth of Forth on 21 August 1997. She was recycled at Alang in 2010 having been renamed *Traveller* for her final voyage.

(Patrick Hill)

There were similarities between some of the Type 104 ships and the solitary Type 128. The latter was launched on 16 March 1984 and delivered as *Kirsten* to Klaus Schneider, of Stade, on 28 April. In mid-December 1988 she was sold to Paul Häse, also of Stade, who owned the china clay slurry tankers. Soon after purchase she too was fitted with slurry tanks and was renamed *Tudor*. This interesting photograph, taken at Par on 12 September 1995 as she awaited departure to St Etienne-du-Rouvray, allows a comparison to be made between her and the Type 104b *Eldor*. Having been built for Paul Häse, *Eldor* has his logo on her bow whereas *Tudor* has only his houseflag. The slurry tanks were removed when she was sold and renamed **RMS Homberg** in 2002, later becoming **RMS Riga** in 2006. She was eventually recycled at Klaipeda in September 2013.

(Cedric Catt)

The twelve examples of Type 129 were built for various German owners between 1985 and 1991. The first one in the series was launched on 19 October 1985 and delivered as **Uwe Kahrs** to Johann Kahrs, of Stade, on 23 November. She and the two subsequent deliveries had a 341TEU capacity but the later examples had a capacity of 374TEU. Once again all the ships of the type were popular with charterers and in September 1986 she was renamed **Gracechurch Gem**, reverting to her original name in February 1988. When photographed leaving Portsmouth in July 1988

she was trading from Antwerp and Rotterdam to Iberian ports with a call at Le Havre and Portsmouth on the return voyage. In October 1989 she was renamed **Maersk Tinto**, reverting to **Uwe Kahrs** in late January 1990, **Maersk Tinto** in May 1990 and then **Meteor** in November 1991. A sale to Dutch owners saw her renamed **Fenja** in 1995 and she became **Sea Vita** for Latvian owners in December 2004. She was acquired by owners in eastern Russia and renamed **Avrora** in June 2008 and since then has traded from that area to China and Japan.

(Bernard McCall)

The final four ships of Type 129 were built for Finnish owners and were designated Type 129a. They were built with additional hull reinforcement which allowed them to be classified as Finnish ice class 1A. The third of the four was *Klenoden*, built like her two earlier sisters for Rederi AB Engship based in the Finnish port of Nagu. She was launched on 20 August 1991 and delivered on 4 October. Seen on the Kiel Canal on 12 August 2007, she was maintaining a service linking Hamburg to Helsinki and Mäntyluoto in Finland. In 2014 she was sold to Egyptian owners and renamed *Leo I*. Since that time, she has traded exclusively in the Black Sea and Mediterranean.

(Dominic McCall)

The Type 130 design was a development of the Type 110 and all five examples of the basic design were built in 1985. They were built for river/sea trading and have just one deck below the bridge and collapsible masts. They have a modest 153TEU container capacity. The **Leeswig** was the fourth in the series and, launched on 18 June 1985, was delivered to Claus Jürgens as **Claus Jürgens** on 20 July. She was sold within Germany in 1993 and renamed **Leeswig**. We see her arriving at Great Yarmouth from Hamburg on 19 September 2006. Later in the year she was sold to Cardiff-based Charles M Willie (Shipping) Ltd and renamed **Celtic Pioneer**. Sold in 2014 she was renamed **C Pioneer** and became **Muhammet Gumustas 6** in 2018. She trades mainly between ports in Turkey.

(Ashley Hunn)

The solitary Type 130a coaster differs from the earlier examples in having fixed masts and a slightly modified wheelhouse. She was launched on 13 November 1985 and delivered as *Rita* to Heinz-Georg Vöge on 17 December. In September 1995 she was sold to Hamburg-based Meerpahl & Meyer and was renamed *Buxtehude*. We see her as such outward bound from Sharpness. In 2006 she joined other examples of Type 130 coasters in the fleet of Charles M Willie (Shipping) Ltd and she was renamed *Celtic Carrier*. In 2014 she was sold to Turkish owners and renamed *Temel Dede*, becoming *Fatma Imamoglu* following sale in 2015 and *Muhammet Gumustas 5* in the following year. She remains busy in the eastern Mediterranean and Black Sea.

(Bernard McCall)

Two examples of Type 130b were built, one of these being *Petuja* which was launched on 1 December 1986 and delivered on 30 January 1987 to Ernst-August von Allwörden. The *Petuja* took her name from the three daughters of her owner, Petra, Uta and Anja. The distinctive feature of the Type 130b vessels was the three deck superstructure beneath the wheelhouse. The ship was renamed *Domalde* for a charter in 1994 and was sold to a Finnish owner in the following year, being renamed *Dyggve*. A sale within Finland in 2001 saw her become *Nedgard* and in 2010 she was renamed *Nedland* by new owners in Tallinn. She returned to Finnish ownership in 2015 as *Prima Donna*. We see her at the Landguard container terminal in Felixstowe on 5 August 1988 when she was linking the Suffolk port to Zeebrugge.

(Bernard McCall)

The superstructure of the five Type 130c ships was one deck higher than that of the basic Type 130 and enabled them to have a container capacity of 198TEU. The **Celtic Venture** followed a similar career to that of **Buxtehude**. Launched on 12 March 1990 she was delivered as **Johanna** to Heinz-Georg Vöge on 19 April. In May 1998 she joined the Meerpahl & Meyer fleet as **Radesforde** and then in 2006 became **Celtic Venture** for Charles M Willie (Shipping) Ltd. She was handed over at Bremerhaven on 11 August 2006 and was photographed exactly one week later at Warrenpoint having arrived on her maiden commercial voyage with a cargo of grain from Shoreham. In 2016 she was acquired by Turkish owners and renamed **Tahsin Imamoglu**.

(David McNamee)

The Type 132 ships were very different indeed from Type 130. They were multipurpose vessels capable of heavy lifts thanks to two 100-tonne cranes. Twelve of the thirteen examples were built between 1987 and 1996 for brothers Hans & Claus Heinrich, of Steinkirchen, and all were given girls' names. The odd one out did in fact join her sisterships five years after delivery. The ships were all to be operated by Schifffahrtskontor Altes Land GmbH & Co. KG (SAL) which was founded in 1980 in Steinkirchen but which moved to Hamburg in 2013. The ship featured here was launched on 18 November 1991 and delivered as **Annegret** on 10 January 1992. She was renamed **Calypso** in 1998 and **BBC Frisia** in 2000. She became **Roelof** after purchase by Dutch owners in 2007. In 2019 she was sold to Russian owners and renamed **Peresvet**. We see her on the Kiel Canal on 17 October 2018 when on passage from Rostock to Aliaga.

(Oliver Sesemann)

The two Type 133 ships were bigger versions of Type 132 and were equipped with two 120-tonne cranes. The first was launched on 15 February 1986 and delivered as **Conti Nippon** on 12 April, her name indicating that she was trading for Contimar Line. In the following year she became **CPC Nippon** when control moved to Continental Pool Carriers. In March 1993 she and her sistership were acquired by Hans & Claus Heinrich,

owners of the Type 132 ships, and she was renamed **Nippon** in 1996. In 1997 both ships were sold to Herbert Lösing and this ship was renamed **Love Song**. She was photographed arriving at Southampton from Antwerp on 22 March 2007. Sold again in 2008, she became **Nordana Olivia** then **BSLE Pacific** in 2010 and finally **Jaohar Aminah** in 2016. She was recycled at Alang in March 2017.

(Colin Drayson)

The only Type 134 was another vessel not to have been built at the Sietas yard. The **Chemtrans Sirius** was a tanker built at the Krögerweft shipyard at Schacht-Audorf on the Kiel Canal near Rendsburg. She was launched on 11 December 1975 and delivered to German owners in April 1976. We see her in the Houston Ship Channel in July 1983. In 1985 she was sold and transferred to the flag of Panama as **Tol Runner**. On 28 January 1987 she arrived in tow at Istanbul after suffering mechanical problems since leaving Piraeus four days previously.

(Harry Stott, Simon Olsen collection)

Repairs were to be undertaken in Hamburg and she arrived at the Sietas yard on 16 April 1987 under tow by the tug **Hermes**. It was decided to lengthen her while she was at the yard and an additional cargo section was added which increased her overall length from 114 metres to 125.2 metres, her deadweight consequently increasing from 7249dwt to 8041dwt. She returned to service in mid-July 1987. In 1999 she was sold to Turkish owners and renamed **Ivyan**. She was photographed off Tuzla on 21 September 2004. Later name changes saw her become **Pokatfinn I** (2006), **Veesham Pokatfinn I** (2010) and finally **Sea Lion I** (2011). She was beached for recycling at Alang in May 2012.

(Simon Olsen)

The only Type 137 vessel was a container ship with a 503TEU capacity. She was launched as *Carina* on 21 February 1990 and delivered to Hans Peter Wegener as *Containerships III* on 4 April. She was the first vessel to be used in the long-standing partnership between her owner and the Finnish company Containerships OY. Her charter lasted almost ten years and she reverted to her original name in October 1999. In 2013 she became *Corina* for Polish owners but reverted to *Carina* in 2018 when acquired by Maltese operators. She is working in the Mediterranean often between Spain and Morocco at the time of writing. When this photograph was taken she was on a service linking Teesport and Rotterdam to St Petersburg and occasionally Helsinki. We see her in the New Waterway in pouring rain on 27 May 1996 on her way to Bremerhaven which was included in the rotation on this occasion.

(Bernard McCall)

The Sietas yard did not build many tankers but the Hamburg-based company John T Essberger did place occasional orders at the yard. The **Heinrich Essberger** was the first of two examples of the Type 138 design and was the third vessel to bear this name. Launched on 16 May 1986, she was delivered on 17 July. She was fitted with sixteen tanks plus one slop tank and also had heating coils. In 1994 she was renamed **Reno** and reverted to **Heinrich Essberger** in 2008. We see her arriving in the River Tees on 7 June 2009 with a cargo of caustic soda from Bützfleth on the River Elbe. Following discharge, she backloaded aniline for Rotterdam. In 2010 she was sold to Russian owners, renamed **Gektor** and is based in eastern Russia along with her sistership. Both tankers regularly load at the Transbunker oil refinery in Vanino, the only refinery in Russia designed specifically for the production of fuel oil for marine engines.

(Richard Potter)

The solitary Type 139 ship was certainly an interesting one, being constructed for a very special purpose. She was built to transport missile parts and equipment from France to Dégrad des Cannes in French Guiana, a port which also serves as the main base for the French Navy in the Caribbean. She was launched on 16 October 1987 and delivered to Hans and Claus Heinrich as *Ariana* on 15 January 1988. In December 1996 she was sold to Cie Morbihannaise et Nantaise de Navigation which explains the initials MN on her hull and funnel as she passed Terneuzen when outward bound from Antwerp to Genoa on 3 August 2004. Sold in 2005 she

was renamed *Beluga Spirit*, becoming *BBC Egypt* in 2007 for the duration of a charter. She reverted to *Beluga Spirit* in 2008 and became *Thor Spirit* following a sale to Danish owners later that year. Sold in 2011 she became *Agata M* and then *Agat* in 2017. In late October 2017 she was intercepted by the Portuguese authorities off the coast of the Algarve for drug smuggling. Having been abandoned and suffering a list at Lisbon, she was eventually recycled at Aliaga in June 2020.

(the late Willem van Maanen, Simon Olsen collection)

There was only one ship of Type 141. She was ordered by Heinz Corleis and was to be named *Odin* but her name was changed during construction and she was launched as *Polaris* on 4 July 1988 and delivered on 29 September. Although without cargo gear, she is nevertheless a multipurpose vessel. She has a stern ramp and has a 508TEU container capacity. She was photographed in the Nordhafen at Bremerhaven on 24 September 2007 when working on the Stella Line service to Kotka. In 2015 she was acquired by VG-Shipping and renamed *Polaris VG* under the Finnish flag. She continues to trade between ports in Finland and those in northern Europe.

(Richard Potter)

There are four ferries that cross the River Elbe between Wischhafen and Glückstadt, the newest being **Wischhafen** that was launched at the Sietas shipyard on 20 August 1988. It is the only example of Type 143 and can accommodate 400 passengers and 55 vehicles. The crossing is hugely popular, especially during the summer months, as it obviates the need to drive through Hamburg. It is, in fact, the only established crossing of the river between Hamburg and the open sea although there are spasmodic attempts to introduce a ferry between Cuxhaven and Brunsbüttel. At Wischhafen there is a splendid museum dedicated to coasters and the small harbour there hosts a harbour festival once every five years. The **Wischhafen** was photographed soon after leaving the terminal at Glückstadt with the ramp visible at the far right of the photograph. After leaving the teminal, the ferries must make a 180° turn to pass north of the island of Rhinplate.

(Bernard McCall)

The **Mini Star** was the first of three Type 144 ships. They were designed for use on services with mixed loads of trailers, containers, paper and palletised loads. Launched on 29 November 1988, she was delivered on 23 December to Finnish owner Oy Minicarriers Ab, which belongs to Godby Shipping Ab and all three were built for charter to Transfennica. They are equipped with a stern ramp leading to the main deck, a starboard side ramp and two 12-tonne cargo lifts for handling rolling cargo. She was photographed in the Kiel Canal soon after leaving the locks at Holtenau on 1 August 1991 when on passage from Kotka to Amsterdam. In 2003 she was sold to the Wilson Group and was renamed **Wilson Star**. She reverted to **Mini Star** in 2015 but was soon trading far from the Baltic. After working on the Mexican coast she moved in 2020 to the eastern Mediterranean and Black Sea.

(Bernard McCall)

The two ships of Type 144a have no side ramp but a closed upper deck without hatch covers. The **Midas** was commissioned by the Finnish company Rettig Ab to be chartered out to Bore Line. She was delivered to Rettig as **Bore Sea** on 9 March 1990. In 2000 she was transferred to the ownership of Oy Minicarriers Ab for operation by parent company Godby Shipping. Like all such vessels operated by the company she has proved to be very popular with charterers. In November 2020 she was time-chartered by Florida-based Accordia Shipping to trade between ports in the USA and the Caribbean. We see her heading east on the Kiel Canal on 12 August 2007 on passage from Bremerhaven to Hamina. At the time she was on a regular service linking Hamina and Rauma to Rouen, Amsterdam and Bremerhaven.

(Dominic McCall)

The six Type 145 ships were delivered in 1989, three going to Rederi AB Engship in Finland and the other three to Oy Langh Ship, also in Finland. They were container ships with a 326TEU capacity. Their reinforced hulls are designed for ice thickness of up to 80 centimetres and meet ice class 1A requirements. The *Winden* was the second of three built for Engship.

She was launched on 15 March 1989 and delivered on 14 April. She was photographed as she passed Cuxhaven on 2 June 2004 on passage from Hamburg and Bremerhaven to Klaipeda and Riga. Later in 2004 she was sold to Cuxhaven-based Guido Buck and renamed ***Ernst Hagedorn***.

(Klaus-Peter Kiedel)

The two Type 145a ships were not container ships but were general cargo ships fitted with two 25-tonne cranes. Both were built for Klaus-Wilhelm tom Wörden and were intended to carry forest products. They entered service on long-term charter to MoDo Distribution, MoDo (Mo och Domsjö) being the third largest forest owner in Sweden. The ships were commercially managed by Navalis Shipping, a company founded in 1995 specifically to support the tom Wörden fleet. The **Hälsingland** was launched on 13 June 1990 and delivered on 14 July. We see her on the Kiel Canal on 27 May 1992. She was sold in 2008 and renamed **Helma**. She left northern Europe in 2013 to trade in the Middle East as **Farah K,** and three years later she was sold to owners in the Philippines for whom she continues to trade as **Span Asia 23**.

(the late John Wiltshire)

Three Type 146 container ships were built for three different German owners in 1990 and a further three for different owners in 1994. Although no sub-group was designated, the second three differed from the first in some details. For example, the first three had four holds and were equipped with two 40-tonne cranes. The second three had six holds and one 40-tonne and one 50-tonne crane. The first ship of the type was launched on 30 July 1990 and delivered as **Widukind** on 10 October. In December 1997 she was renamed **Kent Trader**. In mid-2000 she became **Seaboard Canada** and then **City of Stuttgart** later in the year. We see her passing Battery Point, Portishead, near the end of a voyage from South Africa to Royal Portbury Dock on 17 February 2001. Later in 2001 she was renamed **Perseus**, subsequently becoming **Dubai World** (2004), **2Go 1** (2009) and **Kally C** (2012). She was recycled at Alang in summer 2012.

(Bernard McCall)

The collapse of communism in the Baltic states and Russia led to increased demand for feeder services from ports in northern Germany and the size of the ships soon started to increase. The six ships of the Type 148 design were a development of the Type 129 and had a 510TEU container capacity. The first four were delivered in 1992 and the other two in 1994. The *Uranus* was launched on 23 April 1992 and delivered to Heinz Corleis on 13 June. Charters saw her become *Gracechurch Sun* in 1997 and *Lucy Borchard* in 2002, reverting to *Uranus* in 2005. In 2015 she passed to eastern Mediterranean owners and continues to trade in that area. She was photographed as she passed Grünental on the Kiel Canal on 12 August 2007 on her way to Helsingborg from Hamburg.

(Dominic McCall)

Having been pleased with the performance of its two Type 138 tankers, John T Essberger returned to the Sietas yard for four more tankers six years later. These were designated Type 149 and the final one to be constructed was **Annette Essberger**. She was launched on 3 September 1992 and delivered on 17 December. On 31 January 1997 she was renamed **Alcoa Chemist** and reverted to her original name on 5 September 2008.

We see her off Cuxhaven on 27 March 2011. In 2015 she was sold to Russian operators and renamed **Nordstraum**. In 2020 she was involved in the supply of the Russian fishing fleet, loading in Copenhagen and going to the Barents Sea every time with some calls at Archangel and even visits to the Irminger Sea in the North Atlantic.

(Klaus-Peter Kiedel)

Construction of the three Type 150 ships posed a problem for the Sietas yard. With a beam of 24.50 metres, they would not be able to pass through the Estesperrwerks, the storm barrier which gave access to the River Elbe from the yard and had a width of only 22 metres. The double-hulled ships were built with only a single hull at the Sietas yard and were towed for completion to the Norderwerft yard, then owned by Sietas. Hinrich Sietas campaigned for the barrier to be widened. This work started in 1996 and was completed in 1999. The first two ships were ordered by John-Peter Wulff, of Kollmar, and the first to be completed was **Hermann**, delivered as **Deppe Europe** on 16 April 1993. Space does not permit listing of all her names. She had nine significant charters and reverted to **Hermann** after each of them. She became **Manuela** in July 2006 and retained this name until renamed **Ela** for recycled at Alang in April 2015. We see her as **Manuela** at Laem Chabang in Thailand on 9 May 2014.

(Geir Vinnes)

The 23 Type 151 container feeder ships were built between 1993 and 1998 and were ideal for the rapidly increasing trade between northern Europe and Russia and the Baltic states. Designed for all-year trading to Finland and Russia, they are strengthened to the highest ice class. Not surprisingly, they were immediately popular with Team Lines and Unifeeder and at least seventeen of the type were chartered by one of these companies. They are a development of the Type 129 but they have a beamier hull and they carry a larger proportion of containers as deck cargo. Of the 508TEU capacity, only 143 are carried in the two holds with 365TEU on deck. Two were chartered by K-Line, one of them being *Jan-Fabian* seen here in the Elbe estuary and wearing that company's colours and carrying their containers. Launched on 17 February 1998, she was delivered on 14 March. Sold to Norwegian operators in 2006 she was renamed *Nor Feeder*. She became *A2B Spirit* in 2018 following a sale to Dutch owners.

(Bernard McCall)

The two ships of the Type 152 design were built in 1994/95 for Transportes Marítimos Insulares, a Lisbon-based company which was serving Madeira, the Azores and West Africa from Rotterdam and Lisbon. Since that time, it has extended its services to Asia, North America and northern Europe. The first of the pair to enter service was *Monte Brasil*, launched on 7 June 1994 and delivered on 28 June. The ships have a 636TEU container capacity and are fitted with two 40-tonne cranes. Both ships remain in service under their original names. The *Monte Brasil* was photographed at Ponta Delgada in the Azores on 10 March 2020.

(Tony Hogwood)

The two examples of Type 153 were built for Hamburg owner Hans Peter Wegener. The first was handed over in 1994 and the second was launched as *Wega* on 4 April 1996 but delivered as *Containerships V* on 9 May. They were ice classed container ships with a 749TEU capacity. In 2009 she reverted to *Wega*. In this photograph we see her outward bound in the River Tees on passage to Rotterdam. From there she would sail to St Petersburg and usually included calls at other ports including Helsinki and/or Klaipeda. Both ships later left northern Europe to work on a seven-day circuit from Alicante to Las Palmas and Santa Cruz de Tenerife. In 2020 *Wega* was sold to other German owners and renamed *Charo B*; however she continues to sail from mainland Spain, often Cadiz, to Tenerife.

(Stephen Lowery)

Four ships were built as Type 154. The second two were ordered by Reederei Lehman but the first two were built for Claus Speck, of Rendsburg. The first one was launched on 27 September 1994 and delivered as *Odin* on 28 October. The ships were chartered by Paltrans Shipping, of Västerås, for its service linking ports in western Sweden mainly to ports on the east coast of England especially Goole. They were the maximum size for the Ocean Lock at Goole and had a reduced draft for the shallow sections of the upper Humber and Ouse. Despite this, during neap tides they sometimes called at Hull to lighten before heading upriver to Goole. In 2006 she was taken over by Gothenburg-based Transatlantic Container Shipping and renamed *Trans Odin* but she continued to work on the same route. Transatlantic moved the UK port to Hull and in October 2013 the service was taken over by Sun Line, another Swedish company and the ship reverted to her original name. Along with sister ship *Frej*, she continues to serve the route she was designed for. She was photographed as she passed Cuxhaven on the evening of 19 August 2019.

(Klaus-Peter Kiedel)

Only two ships of Type 155a were built, both ordered by Harry Bröhan and both winning a charter for three years to Hamburg shipping company Deco-Line Peter Determann even before their keels were laid. They were container ships with a 910TEU capacity and had two 30-tonne cranes. Because the Neuenfelde yard was so busy at the time, construction of the *Osnabrück* was outsourced to the Norderwerft shipyard in Hamburg. She was the first ship built by Norderwerft since 1980 and the last of all built by the yard She was launched on 19 October 1996 and delivered on 8 November. Three days later she took up service on Deco Line's service to West Africa from Hamburg to Abidjan, usually calling at Felixstowe, Antwerp, and Dakar, and at Amsterdam on the return journey. She is seen at Hamburg on 11 May 1998. Chartered in July 1998 to the newly-formed West Africa Line (West-Afrika Linien-Dienste), she was renamed *Ubangi* and reverted to *Osnabrück* in 2001. A charter to the Australian National Line saw her become *ANL Progress* in 2003 and she became *Osnabrück* once again on completion of the charter in 2005. In 2012 she was bought by an Indonesian company and renamed *Meratus Batam*.

(Simon Smith)

Two of the three Type 155b ships were built for Quadrant Bereederungs and upon delivery were chartered by Maersk. The **Husky Runner** was launched on 9 December 1996 and completed as **Maersk Helsinki** on 28 January 1997. Both ships have reinforced hulls and have the highest 1A ice classification. The ships have a 942TEU container capacity and this example was delivered without cranes. She was only one month old when photographed at Kiel on 25 February 1997. She was on passage from Aarhus to Europoort on a service linking the Dutch port to St Petersburg and Helsinki with a call at Aarhus on the return to Europoort. In 2002 she reverted to **Husky Runner** and became **Renate P** in 2011. She continues to trade as such in the Mediterranean. Like the Type 150 these ships could not be fully assembled at the Sietas yard because they would not have fitted through the passage of the Estesperrwerks, which was then only 22 metres wide. The double-hulled ships were therefore towed for completion to the Norderwerft yard with the inner hull already closed, but the outer midships section still missing.

(Oliver Sesemann)

The five ships of Type 156 were delivered in two batches. The first three were built in 1995 and the last two were not delivered until autumn 2000. They had a 660TEU container capacity and were all ice-classed 1A. The final one in the series was launched as *Jessica* on 5 November 2000 but delivered to Gerd Bartels as **Lucy Borchard** on 2 December. She worked on the Borchard Lines service from Tilbury, Antwerp and Rotterdam to the eastern Mediterranean. On completion of the charter in 2002 she was renamed *Jessica* then almost immediately *Jessica B*. Under this name she traded initially from Antwerp and Rotterdam to Belfast and Dublin but later from Gothenburg to Bilbao with various intermediate ports. When photographed at Oldenbüttel on the Kiel Canal on 8 August 2007, she was heading for St Petersburg from Hamburg. In August 2016 she was sold to the Russian Kamchatka Shipping Company, renamed **Ivan Kapralov**, and has been used on the liner service between Vladivostok and Petropavlovsk-Kamchatsky.

(Dominic McCall)

There were three Type 157 ships and all were built for charter to Team Lines. The first two were built for Jens & Waller, of Hamburg, and the third for the Koppelmann brothers, again of Hamburg. They had a 326TEU capacity and a 1A ice classification. The **Helene** was the first of the trio and was launched as such on 2 May 1995. She was delivered as **Nyland** on 1 June, all three being given the names of Swedish areas either on or soon after delivery. The **Nyland** was photographed on the Kiel Canal on 12 August 2007 when operating a shuttle service linking Hamburg and Bremerhaven to Muuga near Tallinn in Estonia. In May 2008 she was sold to the Holwerda shipping company of Heerenveen in the Netherlands and renamed **Anja** the following year.

(Dominic McCall)

The three Type 158 ships were built in 1996 for Finnish owner Hans Langh who already had three Type 129 vessels in his fleet. The *Marjatta* was the second of the three and was launched on 30 September 1996 with delivery on 9 November. She was named after the owner's wife. Although they were designed mainly for the container trades with a 468TEU capacity and ice-classed to permit Baltic trading in winter, they were also suitable for the carriage of steel produced in Finland. She was photographed heading east on the Kiel Canal during a voyage from Raahe to Hamburg on 29 May 2005. In January 2009, *Marjatta* made her first transatlantic voyage delivering steel coils from Raahe to New Orleans. She continues to trade from Finnish ports and in mid-2021 was working between Tornio and Dordrecht.

(Bernard McCall)

Construction of the two Type 159 ships began at the Elbewerft shipyard in Boizenburg. In fact this vessel was launched on 24 June 1997 but the shipyard's bankruptcy prevented completion. Both ships were taken to the Sietas yard for completion and the **Margareta B** was the first to be delivered, this being on 9 January 1998. She has a 523TEU capacity. For most of her career in northern Europe she was on charter to BG Freight Line, a company based in Rotterdam which provides a feeder service from that port and Antwerp to other ports such as Grangemouth, Dublin and Tilbury. We see her in the New Waterway on 11 July 2002 outward bound from Rotterdam to Grangemouth. In 2015 this ship was sold to owners in Romania and renamed **Jaohar Rima**. In 2020 she was linking Constanta to ports in the Mediterranean.

(Dominic McCall)

The thirteen Type 160 container ships were built between 1996 and 1999 and were a partial open-hatch design, the third of the four cargo holds having no hatch covers. They had a 700TEU capacity with 100 reefer connections. The second in the series was **Sven**, launched on 20 May 1996 and delivered to Wilfried Rambow, of Drochtersen, on 21 June. Briefly renamed **Solid** on 20 December 1996 she became **Lucy Borchard** on 21 February 1997. She worked on the Borchard Lines service from Tilbury, Antwerp and Rotterdam to the eastern Mediterranean for three years until replaced by the Type 156 vessel of the same name (see page 96 for details of this type). She then reverted to her original name of **Sven** and was photographed on the Kiel Canal heading from Hamburg to Copenhagen and Aarhus on 4 November 2007. In 2019 she was sold and renamed **Dubai Alliance**, trading exclusively in the Middle East since then.

(Neil Burns)

A further seven ships of Type 160a were strengthened for winter Baltic trading and had a Finnish ice class 1A classification. They had a more modest container capacity of 658TEU. Two of the seven were built for Dutch owners and the other five for separate German owners. Mostly they were chartered by Unifeeder or Team Lines. The **Svealand** was launched as *Hanni* on 9 October 1998 and delivered to Jürgen Ohle, of Hamburg, as **Svealand** two months later. She was photographed on the Kiel Canal on 13 August 2007 when serving the Finnish ports of Rauma and Turku from Hamburg and Bremerhaven. She reverted to her original name of **Hanni** when she arrived in Hamburg on completion of this voyage and continues to trade between north German ports and the Baltic.

(Dominic McCall)

Ten examples of Type 161 were delivered between 1997 and 2004. There were four basic Type 161 ships, four of Type 161a and two of Type 161b. The only difference was in the lifting capacity of the three cranes. All were built for brothers Hans and Claus Heinrich for their Schiffahrtskontor Altes Land (SAL), based in Steinkirchen, and all had girls' names. To illustrate the class, we have a photograph of **Annegret**, an example of Type 161a, and she is seen off Kiel on 16 August 2017. The two cranes on the port side each have a lift capacity of 320 tonnes and the stern crane has a capacity of 200 tonnes. She was launched on 29 January 2000 and delivered on 18 March.

(Oliver Sesemann)

The only Type 162 ship was launched as **Concordia** on 10 November 1997 and delivered to Gerd Koppelmann on 5 December as **Chiquita Las Americas** for charter to Chiquita. She soon settled into a trading pattern which saw her trading from Puerto Cortes in Honduras and Puerto Barrios in Guatemala to Miami. She reverted to **Concordia** in 2000 and then spent several years trading along the Norwegian coast. In 2007 she was renamed **Tiznit** for a charter to International Maritime Transport Corporation, a Moroccan company which collapsed in 2013. She reverted to this name after a brief spell as **Concordia** in 2009 but she became **Concordia** once again in 2010. In January 2020 she was sold and renamed **Rainer D**. She has a container capacity of 864TEU of which 232 have reefer connections. She also has two 50-tonne cranes. She was photographed on the New Waterway on 20 May 2016 when she was chartered for the North Sea Container Line service to northern Norway.

(Richard Potter)

The first two ships of Type 163 were ordered by Finnish companies for charter to Transfennica which was established in 1976 as a liner-shipping carrier serving ports in the North Sea and Baltic. In 2002 Transfennica became part of the Amsterdam-based Spliethoff Group. The *Mistral* was the first of Type 163 vessels and was launched on 20 November 1998 with delivery being made on 2 February 1999 to Oy Minicarriers Ab, part of Godby Shipping Ab. From 2004 Godby Shipping used the *Mistral* for UPM-Kymmene between Rauma and Santander. In 2014 she began a five year charter to P & O and worked on various routes but mainly on the Tees to Zeebrugge service. From January 2020 she traded for Balearia between Huelva, Tenerife and Las Palmas. At the time of writing (mid-2021) she was trading between the Danish port of Hirtshals and Tórshavn (Faroe Islands) and Thorlakshofn (Iceland). She was passing the Grünental bridge when heading west along the Kiel Canal on 20 September 2008.

(Oliver Sesemann)

Four of the seven Type 163 ro/ro ships were built for Hamburg-based Ernst Russ as Type 163a and all were chartered to Transfennica. The **Caroline Russ** was the third of the four. She was launched on 3 June 1999 and delivered on 30 June. We see her on the Kiel Canal on 11 August 2007 when she was operating a liner service between Tilbury and the Finnish port of Hamina. The Type 163a vessels were fitted with more powerful engines than the basic Type 163 to enable them to do this round trip within one week. Between January and September 2016 she was renamed **Corsica Linea Dui** for a charter in the Mediterranean. The Ernst Russ company was established in 1893 and despite heavy losses in both world wars, it has continued to prosper and is now a very successful investment company with a focus on shipping and real estate.

(Dominic McCall)

This type was a development of the Type 153. All three ships of the type, delivered between 1996 and 2006, differed and were identified as Type 164, 164a and 164b. The Type 164a seen here was four metres longer than the basic type. She was launched on 14 September 2002 and delivered to Containerships on 1 November as **Containerships VII**. She soon entered service linking the River Tees and Rotterdam to Helsinki. In recent years she has also been calling at Riga. We see her leaving the River Tees on 11 February 2019.

(Stephen Lowery)

The basic Type 164 and Type 164b were built for Hans Peter Wegener but were delivered for charter to Containerships and this Type 164b, although launched as **Mira** on 13 November 2005, was delivered on 7 January 2006 as **Containerships VIII**. The size and layout of the hatches of Type 164b were optimised for the transport of 45-foot containers, so that these special-size containers could be stowed not only on deck but also in the holds. Because of this, her capacity is 850TEU compared to the 966TEU of her two near-sisters. She was photographed arriving in the River Tees from Klaipeda on 7 August 2007.

(David Williams)

John T Essberger returned to the Sietas yard in 1999 and ordered two more tankers that were designated Type 165. This was the company's third order at the shipyard and the design is a development of the Type 149. The second of the pair was **Christian Essberger** which was launched on 30 August 2000 and delivered on 9 November. Each ship had fourteen stainless steel tanks. Until 2017, both ships were painted throughout in a red livery but by the date of this photograph, 30 June 2018, the upperworks were painted white. She was photographed when outward bound in River Scheldt.

(Roger Hurcombe)

This solitary Type 166 ship was launched as *Louise Russ* on 11 December 2000 but delivered on 28 December as *Porto Express*. On 27 January 2001 she was chartered by RoRo Express for trade between Southampton, Leixoes and Tangier. Her speed of 22 knots enabled her to make a round trip in a week. In the autumn of 2001 the charter was unexpectedly ended and she was renamed *Louise Russ* at Hamburg on 25 October. She then had various spot charters but by spring 2002 she was working between Rotterdam and Immingham. Her subsequent career saw her trading throughout northern Europe and occasionally in the Mediterranean. We see her in the River Thames on 21 July 2008 when she was linking Tilbury and Zeebrugge. She was sold to Italian owners and renamed *Eliana Marino* in 2016. In mid-2021, she was trading between the Livorno and Genoa and Sardinian ports of Cagliari and Olbia.

(Derek Sands)

The Type 167 certainly introduced a very different profile to the Sietas output. They were self-discharging bulk carriers and three examples were built. The first was **Stones** which was launched on 17 April 2001 and delivered to Hans-Jürgen Hartmann on 23 May. Herr Hartmann had established the Elbe-Weser-Handelskontor trading company in 1978 and this took over Mibau Baustoffhandel in 1987 (Baustoffhandel meaning building materials trade). The shares of Stema Shipping, a Danish company, were acquired in 1994. We see the ship arriving at Sunderland from Jelsa on 19 October 2013. She was delivering a part cargo because of draught restrictions at Sunderland. In 2015 the ship was sold to a subsidiary of Canada Steamship Lines and was renamed **Donnacona**. She was transferred to the Australian flag and now trades along the coast of Australia.

(Richard Potter)

Two of the 30 Type 168 ships were chartered from new by Orient Overseas Container Line (OOCL). One of these was the appropriately-named **Neuenfelde** which was launched on 11 May 2001 but delivered to Gerd Bartels as **OOCL Neva** on 15 June. The forerunner of Orient Overseas Container Line was Orient Overseas Line established by the late C Y Tung whose dream of creating the first international Chinese merchant fleet was achieved in 1947 when the first ship with an all-Chinese crew reached the Atlantic coast of the USA and Europe. The advent of containerisation saw the company renamed Orient Overseas Container Line in 1969. The ship reverted to her original name of **Neuenfelde** in 2012. She was photographed on the Kiel Canal on 12 August 2007 when on passage from St Petersburg to Antwerp.

(Dominic McCall)

The eleven Type 168a container ships differed from the basic Type 168 vessels in being not ice classed but rather were fitted with two 40-tonne cranes making them more suitable for worldwide trade. As a consequence they have been far less frequently seen in northern Europe. Despite that, **BF Esperanza** was photographed on the Kiel Canal on 28 April 2017 when heading eastwards from Bremerhaven to Helsingborg. Unusually she was only completed at the Sietas shipyard, earlier building work having been carried out at the Daewoo-Mangalia shipyard in Romania. She was launched as **Pioneer Sea** on 14 November 2002 but was delivered as **Maersk Freeport** on 6 March 2003. She became **BF Esperanza** in 2009.

(Oliver Sesemann)

There were eleven examples of Type 168b. They were neither ice classed nor fitted with cranes. The hull of *Stina* was also built by Daewoo-Mangalia and launched on 22 September 2003. She was delivered as a Type 168b on 11 March 2004. Many of this type were chartered by Gracechurch or the associated Borchard Line. This vessel had the distinction of being chartered by Borchard on three occasions – and with a different name each time. She entered service as **Charlotte Borchard** and she is seen as such at Rotterdam on 4 August 2005. She reverted to *Stina* in early April 2006 but in 2009 she became **Rachel Borchard** and then *Stina* again in 2013. In 2016 she was renamed **Katherine Borchard** and in mid-2021 she was working on Borchard's west coast UK service linking Liverpool and Dublin with ports in the Mediterranean.

(Derek Sands)

Six of the basic Type 168 design were later lengthened by 15 metres in 2007/2008 and this increased their container capacity from 868TEU as built to 1008TEU. They were identified as Type 168V or 168L. An example of this type was **Ida Rambow**, launched on 15 June 2007 and delivered on 14 September. She was photographed as she passed Kudensee on the Kiel Canal on 23 October 2011. Not only is there a cross-canal ferry at this location but also sidings where ships can wait to allow the safe passage of other ships. The ferry berth and some of the mooring dolphins are clearly visible beyond the ship which continues to trade between northern Germany and Baltic and Scandinavian ports.

(Klaus-Peter Kiedel)

The four Type 169 container vessels had a 735TEU capacity and were built for Hamburg owner Quadrant Bereederungs GmbH; all were chartered by Gracechurch Lines upon delivery in 2002. This ship was launched as *Pioneer Buzzard* on 8 April and delivered as *Gracechurch Meteor* on 8 June. She reverted to her original name in 2010. She was photographed in the Yangtze River on 29 May 2011. Her usual work at that time saw her trading out of Shanghai, usually to Kobe. Sold and renamed *Conmar Delta* two years later, she became *Harbour Star* in 2018. In 2021 she was trading in the Far East, generally between Hong Kong and Brunei.

(Simon Smith)

There were twelve examples of Type 170, the first four being the basic examples ordered by a Cypriot company for charter to Maersk. They were fitted with three 45-tonne cranes, had a 1678TEU container capacity and reinforced hulls giving them a 1a ice classification. This vessel was launched as **Starlight** but delivered as **Maersk Vigo** on 25 April 2002. Mærsk Line initially put all four ships in the liner service between Algeciras and Santos, also calling at the Brazilian ports of Vitória, Paranaguá and Itajaí. In 2004, the Moroccan International Maritime Transport Casablanca bought the four ships but the charters to Mærsk Line remained unaffected. When that charter ended in 2013, she and two sister ships were arrested for non-payment of wages and laid up in Wilhelmshaven. All three were sold to British company Borealis Maritime and this vessel was renamed **Bomar Victory**. She is seen at Felixstowe on 8 January 2017. Renamed **Victory** for her final voyage she was beached at Alang for recycling on 19 August 2020.

(Derek Sands)

The two examples of Type 170a were ordered by the same Cypriot company, Marlow Navigation, again for charter by Maersk. The first of the pair was launched as **Palomar** on 17 March 2004 and delivered as **Maersk Victoria** on 24 August. Soon afterwards, she was acquired by Peter Döhle Schiffahrts-KG. Both ships ran jointly in a liner service between South Africa and Brazil. The **Maersk Victoria** was then deployed from Manzanillo (Panama) on voyages through the Panama Canal to the US west coast. From 25 July 2008, she operated a feeder traffic between Balboa (Panama) and Esmeraldas (Ecuador). She was renamed **Victoria** in August 2009. We see her passing the Lühe on the River Elbe heading for sea trials on 16 August 2004.

(Florian Horch)

The hulls of both ships were built at the Daewoo-Mangalia shipyard in Romania and towed to Hamburg for completion. The second vessel was launched as **Pyxis** on 13 May 2004 and delivered as **Maersk Vera Cruz** on 27 October. Reederei Döhle had already bought the construction contract for this second ship. The hull was being towed past Cuxhaven on 13 August 2004. She was renamed **Vera D** in November 2009. Both vessels are now trading in European waters with **Victoria** sailing between Antwerp and the Baltic, and **Vera D** between Rotterdam and Iceland.

(Florian Horch)

Like the basic Type 170, the Type 170b has a reinforced hull and was classified ice class 1A. Its superstructure has an additional deck. The higher position of the bridge means that six instead of five container layers can be stowed on the upper deck. Six examples were built, the hull of the first one being built at the Daewoo-Mangalia shipyard as indeed were all the others. The ship was handed over to Peter Döhle as *Safmarine Mbashe* on 10 March 2006. In November 2009 she took her intended name of *Viona* and another charter in June 2012 saw her become *Emirates Dar Es Salaam* before reverting to *Viona* in July 2013. In late 2020 she was sold to German owners Contimar Shipping, renamed *Queen B III* and is currenty trading in the Gulf of Mexico. She is seen in the Kiel Canal at Grünental on 22 August 2013.

(Tim Johannsen)

The solitary Type 171 ship is a gearless container ship with a capacity of 1229TEU and a partial open hatch configuration. Launched as **Oceanex Avalon** on 4 March 2005, she was delivered on 4 May. She usually trades between Montreal and St John's, Newfoundland, for Oceanex. This company was formed in 1990 through the merger of Atlantic Container Express, of Montréal, and Atlantic Searoute Partnership, of Halifax. The previous companies had been providing a shipping service to Newfoundland and Labrador since 1909. The **Oceanex Avalon** was photographed as she passed Quebec on 10 September 2018.

(Klaus-Peter Kiedel)

The first of the eight Type 172 container ships was ordered by Dutch operator Holwerda and the second by Petra Heinrich, of Jork. Construction of the bow and forward section of *Helga* was subcontracted to the Maritim shipyard at Gdansk. The aft section was built by Sietas. The remaining six were ordered by Peter Döhle although the contracts for two of them were transferred to other owners. The first four in the series were chartered from new by Team Lines and therefore had names with the suffix _____land.

The *Helga* was the ship ordered by Petra Heinrich. Launched on 27 January 2003 she was delivered as *Helgaland* on 22 May. In 2013 she was sold and renamed *Page Akia* before reverting to *Helga* in 2017 when sold to Dutch company Holwerda. All ships in the series had a capacity of 822TEU with reefer connections for 150 containers. We see *Helgaland* on the Kiel Canal on 13 August 2007 when on passage from Hamburg to Helsinki

(Dominic McCall)

In the early 2000s, the Icelandic shipping company Samskip awarded the Sietas shipyard the construction contract for two container ships equipped with two 45-tonne cranes that were to be used on scheduled services to / from Reykjavík. The ships were owned by the Bremen-based holding companies. The *Helgafell* was the second of the pair, being launched on 20 December 2004 and delivered on 24 February 2005. The ships have a 909TEU container capacity with reefer connections for 200 containers.

In 2012, Samskip acquired the ships from the German companies. They are used in weekly alternation on a circuit starting from Reykjavík, whereby they usually call at Immingham, Rotterdam, Cuxhaven, Varberg, Aarhus and the Faroe Islands before returning to Reykjavík. We see *Helgafell* in the outer Humber on 22 May 2018 following her early morning departure from Immingham for Rotterdam on the Samskip Iceland Blue service.

(Richard Potter)

It was in 2004 that the Finnish shipping company Langh Ship Oy awarded the construction contract for two modified units which are designated as multipurpose cargo ships and bear the designation Type 174a. The main difference from the Type 174 is that these vessels have no cranes. Despite being designated as multipurpose vessels, they have a 908TEU container capacity and are fitted with cell guides. The *Aila* was the second of the pair to be delivered. She was launched on 19 January 2007 and handed over on 27 March. Both ships are used on Containerships routes. The *Aila* is seen approaching Brunsbüttel locks on 18 August 2017 on passage from Vuosaari to Rotterdam.

(Richard Potter)

The **Misana** was the first of two Type 175 ships ordered by Godby Shipping for an eight-year initial charter to UPM-Kymmene, a major Finnish forest products company. Soon after they were ordered, it became clear that the demand on the planned route would increase in the future, so the ship's design was modified in 2006 and it was extended by 12.60 metres. The **Misana** was launched on 11 August 2007 and delivered on 19 October. Both ships were put on a service linking Finland to Spain; they loaded in Hamina and Rauma for discharge in Santander and El Ferrol. In 2013 they were sub-chartered to Finnlines which maintained the UPM-Kymmene service to Spain. From early 2016 the ships worked on the Rotterdam – Killingholme route for Stena and from 2018 to early 2020 they traded between Harwich and Europoort. In mid-2021 she was working between Rotterdam and Ardalstangen calling at several Norwegian ports en route. The **Misana** is seen at the Europoort terminal on 7 September 2019.

(Richard Potter)

The four Type 176 ships were built between 2008 and 2009. They are developments of the Type 161 and were once again built for Hans and Claus Heinrich but by this time their SAL Heavy Lift had been joined by Japanese shipping giant K-Line. As with all heavy lift ships ordered by SAL, the two main cranes on the port side are prototypes from the Neuenfelder Maschinenfabrik, a company owned by Sietas. They have a safe working load of 700 tonnes and were the most powerful tower cranes in the world when the ships were commissioned. The third crane on the starboard side has a safe working load of 350 tonnes and was also manufactured by Neuenfelder Maschinenfabrik. The *Trina*, launched on 22 August 2008 and delivered on 13 November, was the third ship in the series; she and the final ship, **Regine**, had a superstructure that was raised by one deck. We see her passing Istanbul on 19 May 2014.

(Adrian Brown)

The *Fitnes* was the third of the three Type 177 vessels. They were self-discharging bulk carriers of 33,130dwt and with a capacity of 26,000 cubic metres in their seven holds. She was launched on 20 November 2009 and delivered to Hans-Jürgen Hartmann on 29 April 2010. Between September and December 2015, all three ships returned to the Sietas yard to be fitted with gas scrubbers to clean exhaust emissions. Like the Type 167 ships, they are operated by Mibau/Stema. She was photographed passing Cuxhaven outward bound from Bützfleth for Jelsa on 11 May 2015. Norsk Stein, a subsidiary of Mibau, has operated Scandinavia's largest quarry in Jelsa, Norway, since 1987. From the Jelsa fjord, north of the city of Stavanger, some 10 million tons of high-quality granodiorite per year is shipped to European markets.

(Richard Potter)

Demand for additional capacity on Baltic container feeder routes continued to increase after 2000 and it was felt that larger vessels were needed. The type 178 was designed to solve the problem and at the time it was considered to be the largest vessel of its type capable of navigating the Kiel Canal and serving the majority of Baltic Sea container terminals. It was marketed as a "Balticmax" design ("Ostseemax" in German). Twelve examples were ordered but only half were built because of the world financial crisis in 2008. The last in the series was ordered by the JR Shipping Group, of Harlingen.

Launched on 7 July 2009, she was delivered as *Elysee* on 5 November. The forepart section of the ship was built in Poland and brought to Hamburg by barge. A charter to OOCL saw her become *OOCL Rauma* in 2012. She was photographed in the Kiel Canal on 20 September 2014. The JR logo is prominent on her fore section and just beneath the wheelhouse is a classic-style nameboard bearing the name *Elysee*. In 2021 she was serving on OOCL's Kotka Express service linking Rotterdam and Le Havre with Kotka and St Petersburg.

(Klaus-Peter Kiedel)

The Hamburg-based construction company Josef Möbius Bau GmbH ordered a suction dredger of Type 180 and one of the Type 180a in the summer of 2008. Subsequently, it was decided to build the two examples as Type 180a which was 13.5 metres longer than Type 180 would have been. The first vessel was named after company chairman **Werner Möbius** and was delivered on 29 October 2010. The second ship, named **Eke Möbius** after the chairman's wife, was launched on 20 April 2012 and delivered on 31 August. The suction pipes of the dredging system reach depths of up to 35 metres and the pumps are designed so that the entire ship can be loaded in just under an hour. The pump speed is controlled by a gearbox and a frequency converter continuously reduced to 204 or 141 rpm. The low pump speed is set when excavating and the high speed when discharging the dredged material. Two smaller centrifugal pumps provide pressurised water in order to ensure good liquefaction of the dredged material. In 2016 both dredgers were sold to Boskalis Westminster and in the following year this vessel was renamed **Medway**. We see her at work off Harwich on 26 November 2020.

(David Hazell)

Wyker-Dampfschiffs-Reederei (WDR) celebrated its 125th anniversary in 2010 with the christening of its latest ferry, the double-ended **Uthlande**, the only example of Type 182. She was launched on 23 April 2010, delivered on 28 May and entered service on 15 June. Driven by four Voith-Schneider propellers, she is WDR's biggest ferry to date carrying up to 1200 passengers and 75 cars on five 2.5m wide lanes for a total of 270m. That is one-third more than on the owner's previous ships. Being a double-ended ferry saved a valuable ten minutes on turnround time in port and thus saved fuel costs. Vehicles access at bow and stern at the same time as passengers enter and leave via side entrances at deck level. She was photographed on 19 August 2010. Uthlande is Low German for "the outer lands." She serves between Dagebüll, Wyk auf Föhr, and Amrum, among the North Frisian islands of Germany.

(Bernard McCall)

The story of the two Type 183 ships is not a very happy one. In December 2005 SAL ordered two further Type 176 ships, each of which was to be fitted with two 1000 tonne cranes and dynamic positioning system. The two newbuildings were designated as Type 179. In 2006 two further Type 179 newbuildings were ordered and the first two vessels were laid down on 20 December 2007. Delivery was scheduled for all four during 2010. In August 2008 SAL cancelled all four contracts because of the sharp rise in steel prices. However in summer 2009 it seemed that the global economic crisis was coming to an end and SAL decided to continue the construction of the two vessels already laid down. These were now designated as Type 183. The *Lone* was the second of the pair and was launched on 26 December 2010 with delivery coming on 11 March 2011. She was photographed on the Kiel Canal on 22 June 2018 when on passage from Cartagena to Kemi in Finland.

(Oliver Sesemann)

From the port of Norddeich in north-west Germany ferries serve the islands of Juist and Norderney, two of the seven inhabited East Frisian islands. Much of the freight in recent years has been handled by a dedicated cargo vessel and since 2010 this has been *Frisia VIII* which is the only Type 184 vessel from the Sietas yard. She was handed over on 14 October 2010 and christened exactly two weeks later. More high-sided than the older *Frisia VII*, she can accommodate bulky loads in addition to heavy road vehicles. In March 2012 she was the first ship to be awarded the Blue Angel for environmentally friendly ship design because of the use of a particle filter and an exhaust gas treatment system. The Blue Angel is an environmental label awarded in Germany since 1978 for particularly environmentally friendly products and services. The ship is seen at Norddeich on 19 July 2016.

(Marcus Schröder)

The story of the Type 185 ships is another unhappy one. Three double-ended ferries were ordered at the beginning of August 2010 by Nordic Ferry Services A / S which became Danske Færger on 1 October 2010. The first in the series was **Samsø**, to be used from November 2011 between Hou in Jutland and Sælvig on Samsø. The original owner of **Samsø** was Samsø Linen A / S, which entered into an agreement with Nordic Ferry Services (NFS) in 2008 and wanted to charter the new ferry from the NFS for ten years. The **Samsø** was floated out on 30 July 2011 and completed her first trial in October. She was christened on 4 November 2011 at Norderwerft, part of the Sietas Group, and was due to be delivered shortly afterwards. There was then a dispute between the municipality of Samsø and Danske

Færger, following which Samsø built its own ferry. As a result, Danske Færger postponed the acceptance of the ferry. On 17 November 2011, the Sietas shipyard filed for bankruptcy, whereupon the completed **Samsø** remained in Hamburg. In February 2012, Danske Færger decided to take over the ferry as owner and use it instead of the third ship that had been ordered for the liner service between Spodsbjerg and Tårs. It was given the new name **Lolland** on 23 February 2012. At the same time, the shipping company, in agreement with the insolvency administrator of the Sietas shipyard, cancelled the construction contract for the third ferry.

(Bent Mikkelsen)

The second Type 185 ferry was floated out on 15 April 2012 and completed her first trial on 5 May. The delivery took place on 24 May 2012. The ship was named *Langeland* on 8 June in Nakskov and on 10 June put on the route between Spodsbjerg and Tårs. The superstructure of the third ferry was delivered from Gdansk in October 2011. After the cancellation of the construction contract on 12 February 2012, the insolvency administrator of the Sietas shipyard decided to combine the existing superstructures and hull sections into a floating shell. This was floated out in July 2012 and then remained as part of the bankruptcy estate in Hamburg-Neuenfelde. In July 2015, a Greek owner bought the half-finished ship, which was then named *Dami*. The shell was delivered to the Greek island of Salamis where it arrived on 11 September 2015. It has remained unfinished in the port of Ampelakia.

(Bent Mikkelsen)

The decision of the German government to opt out of nuclear energy was a boost to the offshore industries. The transport of wind turbines to the North Sea, along with their installation and maintenance, would require a significant number of specialised vessels. In December 2010, the Sietas yard received an order from the Dutch Van Oord Group for the first offshore transport and installation ship to be built in Germany. However, Sietas filed for bankruptcy in mid-November 2011 with construction already planned. The sale of the yard to the Dutch VeKa group fell through and the yard was managed by a bank and insolvency board. Van Oord confirmed the order in February 2012 and construction began two months later with completion in 2014. Designated Type 187 and named **Aeolus**, the highly specialised ship has a crane capable of lifting 900 tonnes and capable of working 120 metres above the surface of the water. The vessel can work in water up to 45 metres in depth and can accommodate 74 people. The **Aeolus** was inbound to Eemshaven on 2 August 2015.

(Frits Olinga)

The first of the two Type 190 vessels is **Elbphilharmonie**, a passenger ferry built for work on the River Elbe in Hamburg for HADAG which operates 25 ferries in the city. The vessel is the largest in the fleet and can accommodate 400 passengers with 154 seats on the lower deck, 88 on the upper deck in addition to standing space. Technologically advanced, she has a hybrid drive system with two fixed propellers and two rudders. She also has an exhaust gas cleaning system with two soot particle filters and two catalytic converters. She is named after the Elbe Philharmonic Hall, one of the largest concert halls in the world and opened on 11 January 2017, the year that the **Elbphilharmonie** entered service. The photograph was taken on 16 March 2020.

(Marcus Schröder)

The years following the bankruptcy have been difficult. The decision to cease series production of container ships had already been made and the intention was to concentrate on one-off specialised vessels. Several initial orders were cancelled and the yard began to build sections for the large cruise ships being constructed at the Meyer shipyard in Papenburg. Type 191 is a hopper/suction dredger named *Osterriff* which was ordered by Generaldirektion Wasserstraßen und Schifffahrt (General Directorate of Waterways and Shipping). Ironically the dredger was held up at the shipyard because a build-up of silt prevented her release into the River Elbe. A temporary solution was achieved but it is reported that the silt poses a real problem for shipbuilding at the Sietas yard This photograph of *Osteriff* was taken on 14 June 2021 as she was fitting out at the Blohm & Voss shipyard in Hamburg.

(Tim Johannsen)